CRUISING CONFESSIONS

My adventures working on a cruise ship

by

Harry Greenlee

Cruising Confessions
A Novel By Harry Greenlee

Copyright © 2021 by Harry Greenlee

An
Irish Toast

There are good ships
And wood ships,
Ships that sail the sea,
But the best ships
Are friendships
And may they
Always be.

CONTENTS

FOREWORD

For anyone who ever wanted to know what goes on behind "Crew Only" doors on a cruise ship, this book will give you a no holds barred insight into the amazing world of cruising on the high seas from someone who worked on several cruise lines for over 15 years.

From the complex life of working with people from 42 different countries to romance, drugs, money, and death on the high seas, this book will take you on an amazing journey with true stories and actual experiences that I encountered throughout those 15 years. Some names were changed throughout the book, and the ships mentioned are the same ones I worked on; however, with over 200 cruise ships around the world carrying over 200,000 crew members and over 20,000,000 passengers per year, these stories could have happened on any one of these ships.

I would like to thank all of the crew members with whom I sailed throughout my years working on the high seas. Without them and all of our experiences, I could not have written this book, and to the future sailors who are interested in working on a cruise ship, my advice is to "just go do it," because you will have a blast. I promise you.

Harry Greenlee

DEDICATED

To all of the crew members who sailed with me, and to my
dear friend and colleague, Denzil,
who left us way too early this year. Rest in peace, my good
friend.

Acknowledgments

I would like to thank David Housel, my friend and mentor, who encouraged me to complete
my first book. I would also like to thank Beth Rodgers (BethRodgersAuthor.com), my editor.
Without her expertise and professionalism, this book would not have come to life. I'm
indebted to her, and can't recommend her enough. It was a pleasure working with her.

CHAPTER I

The Journey Begins

Looking back on my life, it was inevitable that I would end up working on a cruise ship. After all, my favorite subject in school was geography. The first book I read was Treasure Island, and I remember at an early age dreaming of floating above the ocean, looking down on tropical islands and sandy beaches. It was not long before my dreams became reality.

It was a warm, sunny July in Miami; the year was 1980. I walked across the gangway to step into a new adventure. For the first time, I felt I was in the right time and place.

The cruise ship was seven hundred feet long, twenty-three thousand tons, all painted a brilliant white with a blue line along its sides. The first thing I noticed was a semi-circled deck around the smokestack, or chimney. Later, I would discover that this was not only the Viking Crown Lounge some seventy-five feet above sea level where you could get a great view of the ocean while sipping a tropical drink, but it was also the signature trade- mark of the company, Royal Caribbean Cruise Line.

As I stood on the gangway, I could smell the salty sea air and hear the cracking of the ropes that held the ship next to the pier as the cruise ship strained against its own weight. The wind and the sea current were pulling the ship away from the pier, like it was trying to break free and head for the open seas.

It was my first day of a new job and a new adventure. I remember thinking this must be the feeling everyone before me had when boarding a ship—mixed feelings of excitement about starting a new adventure, and nerves since I didn't know what to expect.

My adventure was only beginning.

Actually, it began several months earlier. I had traveled all the way from Ireland a couple of weeks prior, packed with one suitcase and my life savings of 200 dollars in my back pocket.

My brother saw an ad in the local paper about working on a cruise ship in the Caribbean. He knew I was looking for a better job.

Although I had finished my hotel business apprenticeship and was only twenty-three-years-old when I was running a busy restaurant in the heart of Dublin, I wanted something more. The money was not so great back in 1978, and neither were the opportunities in Ireland. More out of curiosity than anything else, I checked it out.

I called the phone number and spoke to a young girl who worked for Atlas Staff, an employment agency in Dublin; I asked her to tell me more about the cruise line company. All she could tell me was she had sent a young guy out to work as a server for two years. He then returned to Ireland and bought himself a house. From that moment forward, she had my attention. She followed up by saying if I was interested in finding out more, there would be a recruiting manager from the cruise line in Dublin the following weekend. If I liked, she could make an appointment for me to see him. I said, " Please. That would be great," so she made an appointment for 3:00 p.m. the following Saturday.

It was 2:45 p.m. on Saturday afternoon when I walked into the Shelbourne Hotel and asked the front desk clerk where they were conducting interviews. He said, " On the 4th floor, Room 1403." I thanked him and took the elevator upstairs, walked down the hallway towards Room 1403, and saw a line of people waiting outside. A lady handed me a one page application and said I would need to fill it out before anyone would see me. As I started to fill out the form, the door to room 1403 opened and a small man in a black suit, carrying an old black briefcase, smiled and said, " if you dont have any experience in table-side cooking, please don't wait," Almost half of the people who were waiting in line headed for the elevator.

I did some table-side cooking, but only when I was training at the hotel some five years earlier. However, as I found out later, when I joined the ship, it was only a way to eliminate a majority of people and get down to a selected few. We did not in fact do any table-side cooking as servers while on board. It was not until I became a head waiter one year later that we made Cherries Jubilee and Fettuccine Alfredo. However, it got me into Room 1403 where I sat across a small table from a small man with a quiet voice.

" Hi," he said, " my name is Tyree, Mr. Tyree." He asked me a couple of food related questions, and after several minutes passed, he stood up and offered his hand. As I rose to shake his hand, he said congratulations and told me I would need to get a full medical exam and then get a round-trip ticket to Miami and be at the address he gave me on Wednesday, the sixteenth of July, at 10:00 a.m. He handed me a card which read:

Royal Caribbean Cruise Line

Dodge Island

Miami Fl 33132

There was a blue anchor on the card. It was the company's logo.

I was assigned to one of their three ships that would sail out of Miami to the Caribbean. Two of them were on a one-week cruise—the Song of Norway and the Nordic Prince—and the other was on a two-week cruise, the Sun Viking.

I shook his hand one more time and walked out of the room, took the elevator down, and found my way outside to the street. A cold, blustery wind hit me as I thought about how I would be in the warm Caribbean in a couple of months.

A few days later, while I was organizing my plane ticket and getting all of my medical appointments, I met up with a friend of mine, David. We went to high school together; he had also received a position as a chef for the same cruise line, so we went out at the same time. We wanted to spend a week in New York before we went down to Miami to start work. We would be working sixteen hours a day, seven days a week for the next year, so we thought it would be nice to take a mini vacation and see the sights of New York before all of the hard work ahead of us.

We arrived in New York and we were to stay at one of David's ex-girlfriend's apartment on the Upper West Side of Manhattan. After clearing Immigration and Customs, we got a train into the city. Outside of the station, we looked for a taxi. One man came running up to us, and as he grabbed our bags. He said, " Taxi."

I replied, "Yes, thanks." He dropped our bags at the taxi stand and put his hand out. "Five dollars," he said. I reluctantly handed him the $5, and he ran off down the street.

"Welcome to America," David said. We both laughed out loud.

After a few days in New York, it was time to head down to Miami and report for work. Stepping off of the plane in Miami, the heat hit us like opening an oven door. It was 88 degrees Fahrenheit, but with the humidity, it felt like 100 degrees. It was nine in the evening, and the sun had gone down when we grabbed a taxi to take us to the hotel on Biscayne Boulevard. The hotel was old, dilapidated and the rooms were crammed with five or six people, not your five star hotels you read about in Miami, however for a couple of day's it will do.

The next morning before going to the office, I noticed I had misplaced my passport and came to the conclusion that I must have lost it in New York. We went over to the office, anyway; David could start work, but they couldn't send me on the ship without a passport and the visas necessary to work on board.

I had to wait until the Irish Embassy in New York sent me a replacement, and then I would have to go to the Bahamas to get a visa stamped into my passport before I could sail. This entire process took three more weeks. During this time, I was staying in a hotel in Miami. After counting my money, I knew I would only have around three dollars each day to spend on food.

After the third week, I went to the office over on Dodge Island. When I entered the office, I was greeted by a beautiful young girl, a tall blonde in her early twenties. She smiled and said, "Can I help you?"

I replied, "Yes, I would like to speak to the operations manager."

"Who will I say wants to speak to him?"

"Harry," I replied.

She picked up the phone and pressed three digits. She then mumbled a few words and hung up.

"Someone will be out to see you. Have a seat while you wait."

I looked around the room. There was a large photo of the three ships and a plaque that read: "Persistency in excellence is the hallmark for success."

On the wall immediately behind the receptionist was a large photo of a waiter with a big smile, dressed in a red and white jacket and one of those hats you see people wearing during an election with a red, white, and blue band around it. He was holding a large baked Alaska, an ice cream dessert, over his head. Later, I would work with this waiter and little did I know at the time he would have a profound effect on me.

A moment later a door to my left opened, and a tall, portly gentleman with a jovial smile approached me and shook my hand. I introduced myself to him and he said, "I know who you are" in a strong Cuban accent.

I told him to give me my plane ticket and let me go home as I was running out of money. If I could not get on the ship soon, I would be better off going back to Ireland. He replied, "No, we are going to fly you to the Bahamas so you can get your visa."

I said, "But I don't have any money left."

He replied, "Don't worry, we want you to join the ship, so we will take care of this and you can pay us later after you are on board a couple of weeks. Go back to the hotel and wait till you hear from me."

I shook his hand and said, "Thank you."

As I walked back across the bridge from Dodge Island to the hotel, I thought I must have made an impression already or maybe it just was my lucky day. Things seemed to be looking up.

My routine the last week in Miami was the same every day. I got up as late as I could, did without breakfast, walked about a mile to McDonald's and bought a small Happy Meal around 3:00 p.m., then walked back to my hotel and ate my lunch slowly before watching TV and going to bed around 8:00 p.m..

One morning I took a bus ride out to Miami Beach. I wanted to see the famous beach, and then I remembered the hotel in the James Bond movie *Goldfinger*, so I went to see it. The name of the hotel was the Fontainebleau. I even had a drink at its famous pool bar. I remember handing over a ten-dollar bill to the bartender, but he denied it. I didn't want to argue with him, so I produced another ten dollars to try and pay again. *Welcome to America*, I thought.

A few days later, the phone in my room rang. I was hoping it was the office either telling me I was going home or that I was going to the Bahamas to get my visa, but it turned out to instead be a female voice on the other end. She said, in broken English, "Come down to the restaurant. I have some breakfast ready for you."

I tried to say no because of my money situation, but she would not take no for an answer, so I figured I would go down, have a cup of coffee and some toast, and forgo my late lunch at McDonald's.

I got up and dressed, then headed down to the lobby. When I went into the restaurant, a beautiful young lady met me, around twenty-two years old, with long, dark black, silky hair. She was slim and tall with beautiful brown skin. She looked like a model who had just stepped out of a fashion magazine.

With the biggest smile, she said, "Hi, my name is Marie. Please have a seat and I will bring you breakfast."

I sat down at a clean table set up with a white tablecloth, linen napkins, and silver-plated cutlery. As I got to know Marie, she explained to me how she had moved to Miami from Cuba with her mother when she was only two years old. At the time we met, she had been in Miami for twenty years. She spoke English well with a strong Spanish accent, and when she smiled, the entire room lit up. I will never forget that smile as long as I live.

Marie headed off to the kitchen, and a moment later she returned with a glass of fresh orange juice, a full plate of bacon and eggs, hash browns, toast, and a mug of hot coffee. As I tucked in, I told myself I didn't care if the meal used up all of my money; I was going to enjoy it and worry later about how I would take care of myself the next few days. As I scraped up the last morsel of food from my plate and downed the last drop of hot coffee, I asked Marie for the bill. She said, "No, it's okay. This is on me."

I replied, "No, I can't let you do that."

She told me not to worry about it, and that it was her treat.

I thanked her so much and left the dining room full and happy.

At the time, I was not aware that she knew of my situation living on one small meal a day.

The next morning, she called my room again, and so as not to take advantage of her kind generosity, I told her I had to go to the office early that morning and would not have time for breakfast. Instead, I thanked her and hung up the phone.

Two days later, I took a seaplane over to the Bahamas. It took about 30 minutes to fly from Miami to Nassau. We arrived at Paradise Island and then I took a short taxi ride over the bridge separating the island from the mainland and arrived at the Embassy. As I stood in line waiting for my passport to be stamped, I was reflecting on what had happened over breakfast two days earlier and made a promise to myself that with my first paycheck I would buy a nice gift for Marie and present it to her the following Saturday when I got back to Miami after my first cruise.

After a two-hour wait, I got my passport stamped with the necessary visas, C1 and D1, and left for the airport on Paradise Island where the seaplane was waiting to take me back to Miami later that night.

I didn't sleep well that night; I was too excited about what was to come the next day.

CHAPTER 2

All Visitors Ashore

I woke up at 6:00 a.m. on Saturday morning, took a quick shower, and packed for the last time. I looked around the room thinking, *I don't care if I ever see this room again.* I closed the door behind me and walked towards the elevator; I stepped inside and pressed the button for the ground floor to the lobby. As I exited the elevator, and before I went outside, I took a detour to the dining room to see if Marie was there. Sure enough, she was pouring coffee for a couple at a table and she glanced over at me and acknowledged I was there. A short time later, she walked over to me. I put my hand out to shake hers and to thank her for taking care of me while I was there; she did not accept my hand, but reached over and kissed me on both cheeks, whispering "good luck" in my ear. I said goodbye, then turned and walked out of the hotel.

I went over to the office on the pier at Dodge Island to check in, and within an hour I was walking across the crew gangway to enter a new world and the start of my sailing adventure.

I met the crew purser, a heavyset man who looked to be in his mid-forties, dressed all in white with a couple of strips on each shoulder, along with a bit of a beer belly and a funny looking mustache. He took my passport and medical papers, and with a thick Norwegian accent, he said, "Welcome aboard. I will show you a short movie about life on board the ship and hand you a book of rules and regulations to read later. You will receive a life jacket with a small book of instructions, telling you where your station will be in an emergency. I will need you to sign a couple of papers and then I will assign you your cabin."

There were several of us who were signing on that day. Besides myself, there were two young girls, one joining the Purser's Office, and the other was a dancer. There was also one older gentleman who was returning from a vacation to go back to work in the engine room. A total of five of us were joining as waiters. We all met in the crew bar, the only room large enough which was not open in port.

After an hour, another purser showed us around the crew dining room and some of the other crew areas before taking us to our cabins.

I wanted to explore the whole ship, but there were very few passenger areas I was allowed to see. In fact, I spent the first three months just going from my cabin to the restaurant through some back stairs marked "Crew Only," and up seven decks, to the dining room. That was my routine every day. When I asked a fellow waiter some weeks later if he could show me how to get to the crew swimming pool, he replied, "maybe you should wait a couple more weeks. It's hard to explain to you how to get there."

A moment later I was heading to my cabin. The crew purser said something about not having a bed yet in the crew area, so I would have a passenger cabin for the first week. At the time, I didn't have any clue what the difference was.

When we arrived at the cabin, the room number on the door read 405. As he opened the door and entered the room, he said, "Don't get too comfortable here. It's only for a week and then you will be assigned a room down in the crew area." He handed me a key and added, "Don't forget to make your way to the restaurant by 3:00 p.m. The restaurant manager will meet you there, and don't be late." He turned and left, closing the door behind him.

I put my suitcase down and sat on the end of the bed for a couple of moments, surveying my room. It was about twelve feet long and five feet wide with a porthole of sorts; it had a large, round, steel plate covering it. Later that night, when I heard the water splashing at the bulkhead, I realized the cabin was half underwater and that was why the port hole was covered up.

There was a small table and chair against one wall, and at the end of the cabin near the door was a small room with a toilet, hand basin, and a small shower. The bathroom was only four feet by three and a half feet wide; it was so small I remember later how the cruise director said one could take a shower, brush teeth, and go to the toilet all at the same time. By the small bed was a table with a small drawer and a lamp. The room was nice, neat, and practical. In the early eighties, there were no TVs in the cabins and VCRs were still a couple of years away. It was also at that moment when I was alone when I began to feel homesick. Even though I had been away from home before, this was different. Not only were there some three and a half thousand miles between me and my family, but also five hours difference. There were no cell phones or even phone cards at the time, so it wasn't easy to call home, especially while on the ship. You could request a time slot with the radio officer and wait until all of the satellites were in line, then pay him eight dollars per minute, but that was not practical. The best you could do was write a letter which would take two weeks to get there.

I stopped thinking of home and opened my suitcase, took out my clothes that I needed for dinner, and got dressed in a white shirt, black pants, black socks, black shoes, and a black bowtie.

When I finished dressing, it was 2:30 p.m., so I left my room, locked the door behind me, took another look at the room number so I could find it later that night, and climbed seven decks to the restaurant. After climbing the stairs, I pushed open a heavy door and walked into the largest dining room I had ever seen. The dining room was called "The King and I". All three Royal Caribbean ships used famous musicals to name their public rooms.

The dining room was decorated in gold and had several oriental accents. It had some tables of eight and others of six all along the windows on both sides, and in the center there were several large, oval tables, and one extra-large round one right in the center of the room. I later found out that this was the captain's table and only used when he came down for dinner a couple of nights each cruise.

The whole restaurant held six hundred people. There would be two sittings for twelve hundred passengers. We would serve a four-course meal during the first sitting at 6:00 p.m., then vacuum and reset the whole dining room and do it all over again for the second sitting at 8.30 p.m.

There were a couple of waiters over in a corner by a large window, so I decided to go over and join them. I introduced myself and they told me their names. There was Luigi from Italy, Mike from England, Mustafa from Turkey, and Louis from Portugal. More and more waiters arrived until there were around seventy or eighty people sitting in the center of the dining room. Later that night, I found out there were forty-two different nationalities on board the ship, at least among the crew.

Soon after we began talking, a small man wearing a black tux, who had a dark Latin look, entered through the large glass doors at the other end of the room. He approached us with a smile as he turned to look at the five new waiters sitting in the front. He said, "Good afternoon, gentlemen, and welcome to 'The King and I' dining room. This will be your new home for the next year. My name is

Mr. Francisco, and I am the maître d'. Tonight I will assign you each to a waiter. You will work alongside them as a busboy, or commie waiter, as it is known in Europe."

I was assigned to an experienced waiter from Turkey. His name was Hassan, and he was a medium built man in his late thirties with a very thick, broken English accent. He had worked as a waiter on the ship for six years, so I felt lucky to work with someone who had so much experience.

After getting our station ready, the dining room manager gathered all of the waiters and busboys together in the center of the dining room. I counted 80 of us as one of the head waiters did a roll call to make sure everyone was on board and ready for work. The dining room manager said a few words about the last cruise, then told us how many passengers were on the current cruise. He then introduced us, the new guys, to everyone else in the room and said where we were all from, but it was at that moment when there was a loud beep on the speaker system which interrupted the maître d', followed by a voice saying: *"All visitors ashore. The ship is about to sail. If you are not sailing with us, please make your way to the gangway as the ship will depart promptly at 5.00 p.m."*

When the announcement ended, the dining room manager continued saying something about the ratings and comments from the last cruise, then named all of the waiters who made five stars last cruise, which I came to learn more about later on, and then he assigned everyone to their stations for the week. Each waiter would be assigned several tables, along with a busboy, to help him.

Unbeknownst to us at the time, a couple of decks above us the passengers were gathering together for when we sailed away. There were a couple of musicians playing some jovial songs. Each passenger was wearing an orange life jacket, and they were throwing streamers over the side of the ship and letting off balloons. This balloon activity was stopped a couple of years later because it didn't bode well with environmentalists. However, it's a part of the cruise experience I think is sadly missing today.

The sail away had two purposes. One was to get everyone in the party mood, and another more serious one was to have the passengers first and only lifeboat drill. It is a mandatory drill that the U.S. Coast Guard insists every passenger takes before a ship leaves its first port.

Everyone donned their life jackets which they found in their rooms and proceeded up to the lifeboat deck where an officer checked on everyone. It was the only serious part of the cruise for the passengers.

As everyone was assembled on the boat deck enjoying the music, two beautiful blonde girls in red hot-pants and white T-shirts stood on top of a moving cage (something like the machines you see when they are fixing the street lights). They were about fifty feet in the air taking photos of all of the passengers along the promenade deck. The machine moved at a slow pace along the pier a couple of feet from the ship's side. When they got to the other end of the ship, they handed over all of the film reels to a photographer on board who developed the photos while all of the passengers ate dinner. They would be available for viewing and for sale later that same night.

Before the glass doors of the dining room were opened, I heard the iron doors closing one deck below us. The ship started to shudder and creak, then tilt a little to the left. The silverware on the tables rattled as the ship pulled away from the pier. It was a strange feeling at first, but I got used to it pretty quickly. The ship did a complete turn in the bay of Miami and headed out to sea. A couple of miles out, the pilot boat drew alongside the ship. As I watched from the restaurant window five decks above, the pilot was timing the waves before he jumped from the ship to the pilot boat; he looked back up at the captain on the bridge, and as the pilot boat sped away from the ship, he waved goodbye. A moment later, the dining room manager told everyone to get ready. "We are about to open the doors for the first seating. All head waiters stand by the doors and get ready to open."

He disappeared into a small room next to the dining room, and a moment later, at the same time as the big glass doors opened, the dining room manager banged a few notes on a xylophone and then, in a strong Italian accent over the PA system, said: *"Good evening, ladies and gentlemen, 'The King and I' dining room is now open for all of our first seating passengers. Dinner is now being served. Thank you and bon appétit."*

At the same time, a rush of passengers came streaming in from all four sides of the dining room looking for their tables that they had been earlier assigned; it took about ten

minutes for everyone to find their table and sit down.
A couple of families were gathering around the center table
waiting for the dining room manager to assign them a table.
I found out later that they were the last people to board the
ship just before sailing.

Hassan and myself had two tables of eight, and as
soon as all of our passengers were seated, they introduced
themselves to each other. There were two families at one
table of eight, including two sets of parents and four kids—
two girls about eight or ten years old and two boys about
six or seven years old. At the other table there were three
couples. One couple looked like they were in their twenties
and on their honeymoon. Many years later, my wife met
the same couple when she worked in a hotel in Cocoa
Beach. They were about to take another cruise out of Port
Canaveral with their children to celebrate an anniversary.
The other two couples were in their forties, along with a
mother and daughter. The daughter had just turned thirty-
two and was on the cruise to celebrate her birthday. Hassan
introduced himself to everyone and then he introduced me.
I noticed everyone was interested to hear that I came from
Ireland and those who had been there said nothing but good
things about their visits there. I felt very at ease and, for the
first time, proud to be Irish.

Hassan handed out the menus which read "WELCOME
ABOARD DINNER" at the top of each one. While I filled
everyone's glasses with ice water, Hassan took their orders.
Several passengers asked me for iced teas. I didn't know

what that was, as the only tea I knew was the hot cup of tea the English and Irish enjoyed. After Hassan explained to me, I went to the kitchen to get some. Hassan went to get their appetizers. While he was away, some passengers asked me how I traveled from Ireland. The first thing I noticed was how friendly Americans were, unlike in Europe where serving the public in a restaurant is like being a second-class citizen. They appear to always look down on you there, but that was not the case on the ship. I knew at this point that I was going to enjoy my new job.

After Hassan served the starters and then the soup from a large buffet in the center of the room, we headed to the kitchen. He got the main course and I picked up the vegetables.

I lined up with all of the other busboys to get four trays of vegetables and potatoes. As I waited in line, I glanced over to the cooks on the line and I noticed David. He was very busy placing some meat on a row of plates under a hot lamp. He also noticed me, and we briefly nodded to each other. It then came to my turn, and one cook asked me, "How many?" He glared at me, looking for a response. "How Many?" he asked me a second time.

"How many what?" I asked.

"How many guests do you have? And hurry up—you're holding up the line."

I apologized and followed up by saying, "I have sixteen." He then gave me enough vegetables and potatoes for sixteen people. I left without getting a chance to talk to Dave. It would be two days before we had another chance to talk to each other in the crew bar.

I returned to the dining room before Hassan, so I cleared all of the plates from both tables. When he returned with all of the food, he would put them down and I would follow with the vegetables.

I had just cleared the last plate when I saw Hassan coming through the dining room with a large tray on his shoulder with sixteen plates with plate covers. It was about three feet higher than his shoulder, and as he walked through the dining room, he ducked down to avoid hitting the sprinklers in the ceiling. When he arrived at our station, he slowly and with one move put the tray down on his side stand and asked me if I was ready. We then quickly served everyone, followed by dessert, and I served coffee after that. Hassan explained the hours of the dining room and where else you could get food on the ship, then it was time for everyone to leave the dining room so we would have time to reset the tables for the second seating and do it all over again.

After we finished the second seating, it was time for us to get some food to eat for ourselves. I was hungry, as it was almost ten o'clock and I was not used to eating so late. I would soon get used to it, though. At this time, all 80 waiters and busboys would grab their dinner and sit together on one side of the dining room, usually in groups from each country. There were Filipinos at one table,

Italians at another, Turks at another, and so on. I found a seat with a couple of English waiters. I was the only Irish waiter on the ship. We all sat together talking in our own languages.

I was feeling well; however, my feet were tired. I thought we were finished for the day; however, we had still to set up for the midnight buffet. I was pleased to know that there was another crew to work the buffet, so it was off to bed. As I climbed down the crew stairs, Hassan came up behind me and slapped me on the back saying, "Great job tonight. You were like a pro."

"Thanks," I replied.

"Don't worry, it gets easier, you'll see," replied Hassan. "Have a good sleep and I'll see you in the morning and we'll do it all again. Don't be late."

"Good night," I replied, "and thanks for your help, you're an excellent teacher."

As we reached D Deck, Hassan turned off to the left while I went to the right.

I found my way back to my cabin, and after a quick shower and getting into bed, saying a few prayers, and reminiscing about how the day went, my mind went quiet. I drifted off to sleep hearing the waves splashing on the side of the ship and the faint noise from the engines, along with the strange creaks from the wood walls as they strained against the hull shell. Soon enough, I was asleep.

My first week went quickly. My typical day would start at 6:00 a.m. That was the time I would jump out of bed and take a shower. I would make my way up to the dining room by 6.30 a.m. We would get our stations ready for the first sitting breakfast that started at 7:00 a.m., then second seating was at 8:15 a.m., before getting ready for lunch at 12:00 p.m., then 1:30 p.m. Next, there would be a two hour break before getting ready for dinner at 5:00 p.m. to open for the first sitting at 6:00 p.m. We would clean the dining room and reset for the second sitting at 8:30 p.m. We would then get a quick bite to eat ourselves at 10:30 p.m., then set up the room for the midnight buffet which we would all work on Thursdays for the gala buffet. This was the big buffet when all of the passengers would line up to take photos and get to talk to the chef. We would work until 2:00 a.m., then return to the restaurant by the following morning at 6.30 a.m.

By the end of the week, my feet were sore with muscle pain. That too would go away after a couple of months. My feet would throb with pain as I went to bed each night and I would find myself still in pain the next morning. The small muscles in my feet were not used to so much walking and standing, working around 16 hours per day, and we would do this 7 days a week for 9 or 10 months before we could take time off the ship.

Many restaurant servers don't make it to the first month. About 20% will not make it to the end of the first month, and by 6 months, over 50% of the waiters often quit and went home. That's the reason you have to have a return ticket when you start. In fact, out of the other four waiters that started the same day I did, I was the only one who returned for another year.

Each night it was smooth sailing apart from the creaking, cracking, and throbbing of the propellers. I would not have known we were on the high seas except for a small swaying from side to side which helped put me to sleep. A funny thing happens to everyone the first time taking a cruise. After stepping on land for the first time, it feels like rocking from side to side. Your middle ear is trying to help you balance. The ground seems to move. This effect happened to me when I stepped off of the ship in St. Thomas. This was my first taste of land since stepping on board in Miami. I eventually got used to it and after a while, I didn't feel it anymore.

At the end of the cruise, all of the guests received five envelopes, a couple of Immigration and Customs forms, and a comment card to fill out about how they would rate every department on the ship.

The five envelopes included one for tipping the head waiter, one for the waiter, one for the busboy, another for the cabin steward and his assistants, and the last was a blank one they could use for anyone else they felt helped to make their cruise special. There was a little card in each room explaining how much was suggested to put in each envelope. Each couple or family would bring their envelopes to the dining room on the last night to hand out at the end of the meal. I was so excited to see how much I had made my first cruise.

Later that night when I got back to my cabin, I opened each envelope one at a time and arranged the money by denomination. In the first pile I placed the twenties, in the second pile were the tens, then the fives, followed by the ones. After opening all of my envelopes in my cabin later that night, I had $300—that was quadruple my salary from the last job I'd had in Ireland. Quite a lot of money for a weeks work back in the eighties and it was tax free.

CHAPTER 3

The Gift

The next morning was Saturday, the day the ship arrived back in Miami. After breakfast, and after saying goodbye to all of my passengers, the crew purser approached me to say I would move into my new crew cabin, and would I pack my bags and meet him at the crew office at 10:00 a.m.

I arrived with all of my belongings and followed him down two more decks, along a passageway. This time, the carpet changed to linoleum, the long hallway got narrower as we passed a large bathroom with communal showers, and I peered through the door to see there were twelve showers in a row, separated by a shower curtain and six sinks across from them with ten more toilets at the end of the large room. At that point I realized there would not be a shower in my room.

We came to a stop, at cabin C120. He opened the door with a key and then handed it to me. He said, "This will be your room from now on. Keep your life jacket at the end of your bed." I realized we were definitely under water on this level.

It was a little larger than my last room; however, I would share it with three others. There was one bunk bed on either side of the room, with a narrow walkway down the middle. We each had one drawer under the bottom bunk beds and a very narrow locker at the end of the bed for all of our clothes. In the corner was a small sink and a narrow mirror above it for all four of us to share.

They assigned me the top bunk, with a small light above my head for reading at night without worrying about disturbing anyone below. The bed itself had a very thin, hard, horsehair mattress, and it was only three and a half feet wide by five and a half feet long. Although we spent little time in bed, it was very uncomfortable and hard to fall asleep. I never got used to it, and I promised myself, when I eventually left the ship life, I would spend whatever it cost to buy the best bed out there. I thought to myself, if people spend a third of their lives in bed, it better be the most comfortable one money can buy.

I put my stuff away and changed quickly into a pair of jeans and a T-shirt, then headed off to find the gangway. I was on a mission. I went upstairs to the purser's area and found it next to the Purser's Office. When I reached it, a tall, thin gentleman, all in white with gold strips on each shoulder and wearing a white cap, put out his hand to stop me.

"Where do you think you're going?" he asked.

"I'm going ashore," I replied.

"Not here, you're not," he snapped.

"Why not?" I asked.

"This gangway is for passengers only. You must go to the crew gangway."

"And where is that?" I asked anxiously.

"Deck D," he snapped.

He was busy with a passenger, so I headed back downstairs until I found deck D. Then I saw some other crew members and asked them how to find the crew gangway. They told me to follow them.

A few moments later, I arrived at the gangway, and I attempted to step off of it for the second time. I looked to my left, where there was a large board telling the crew what time to be back on board. It read: ALL CREW MEMBERS NEED TO BE BACK ON BOARD NO LATER THAN 4:30 P.M.

This is something you always checked when leaving the ship, because if you were to miss this time and be late, the ship would sail away without you and you would be fire, no questions asked.

As I approached the gangway, another gentleman in a white uniform stopped me and said, "Where do you think you're going?"

I replied, "I'm going ashore."

"Not yet you're not. You're new, right?"

"Yes. Started last week."

"Well then," he said, "you must go through Immigration before you go ashore. You will need to go up to the showroom lounge and meet with the Immigration officer, and then, and only then, you can come back down here to get off the ship."

I rushed up 10 decks to the lounge just in time to collect my passport from the purser, and head over to a table where one surly Immigration officer was seated.

I handed him my passport. As he skimmed through it looking for my photo, then my D1 visa, he looked up at me twice, and back to my photo once again. He stamped my passport and said "Next," then on my way out of the lounge, another purser collected my passport back and told me that the ship would hold on to it as long as I remained on board. I would get it back when I signed off on leave.

I rushed back down to the gangway, to deck D, and as I was leaving again, one officer handed me a small card with my photo on it, as well as my name and the name of the company and ship. It looked somewhat like a driver's license. This would be my boarding pass. He said, "Don't lose it, you will need it to get back on board later."

I had used up two hours of my shore leave, and time was short. As I ran off of the gangway and across the pier to a line of taxis, I grabbed the first one and asked the driver to take me downtown.

The first thing on my mind was, as I had promised myself, to find a store where I could buy something nice for Marie.

The taxi dropped me off at the corner of Biscayne and 1st Street. After walking a couple of blocks, I found a store on 1st Street. It looked like I would find something nice for her there. I ran into the store and searched for the perfume counter, then headed across the street to a flower shop, where I grabbed some tulips and a card. This took me all of an hour, and then, as fast as I could, I ran down Biscayne Boulevard, around a couple of corners to the hotel that I had stayed in for nearly a month. It felt like a prison to me now. I thought about how they had put four or five of us into one room with beds on the floor, and how there were cockroaches running around the floors and over us throughout the night. The rooms smelled, and the bed linens were never changed. It used to be called the "roach hotel" by many.

I went in through the main double glass doors, into the lobby, then left to the dining room, where I saw Marie. She was lifting a few plates off of a table and as she turned, she looked over at me and smiled. Her beautiful brown eyes met mine as I walked over to her and handed her the gift. I said, "Thank you, thank you for everything, Marie."

She looked surprised as she opened her gift and read the card. Her eyes filled with tears as she read

Marie,

I can't thank you enough. You were the first person in America who made me feel welcome and I wish you and your mother good health and happiness.

Harry

Marie leaned over and kissed me on both cheeks. "Thank you," she whispered.

We said goodbye, and I turned and walked out of the hotel, not knowing if our paths would cross again. Sadly, they never did.

CHAPTER 4

Death on the Ocean

My second week started off with a surprise. I arrived early in "The King and I" dining room to set up my station, and then I was sitting in the dining room waiting for the manager to enter and give us our new stations for the new cruise. He would always read out the busboys' names first because that gave them more time to get their stations ready. As he got to the end of the list, I hadn't heard my name called. I wondered if he'd missed me, or if I hadn't been listening and missed it. Right then, he called my name and said, "Congratulations, Harry, you are going to be a waiter this week." Normally it took several weeks, and sometimes months, before you would be promoted, but he saw something in me that convinced him I would make a great waiter. I was nervous, but when I found out they put a very experienced busboy named Luigi with me, I felt better. Luigi was from the north of Italy and spoke broken English, but his personality made up for it. He had been a busboy for five years and did not want to be a waiter because of the pressure of making the ratings every cruise. I would find out more about the ratings system at the end of my first cruise.

Luigi was great and helped me so much my first week as a waiter. He would entertain the guests with songs and stories, as well as tricks for the kids, while I was in the kitchen, and they loved him, I would share him with another waiter, so Luigi would have twenty-eight passengers each sitting. He was fast, and I don't know how he did it, but he could keep up with both of us and didn't miss a beat.

On the last night of the cruise, the head waiter approached me and asked me if I needed help explaining the comment card to my passengers. I said yes, as I didn't know exactly what he meant.

On the last night of the cruise, all passengers received a comment card in their cabins, along with several envelopes for tipping. It was my job to tell them I needed them to mark excellent for the food and service. The trick was to ask them, but not to insist. If they complained that a crew member solicited their responses, and the office found out, that person's job could be lost; however, if it wasn't mentioned, there was a chance for a bad rating and the loss of one's station or, as in my case, I would go back to being a busboy again, and I didn't want that. I enjoyed being a waiter in charge of my station; it was a catch-22 situation.

I spoke to my passengers during both seatings about the rating and if they enjoyed my service and food to make them excellent and that was it. I kept it short as I was also nervous.

I learned later on to perfect my speech and relied on my service to speak for itself. The food was a little different, but I never begged as other waiters did. Some would say if they didn't receive an excellent rating, how they would get a one-way ticket home and could not feed their kids. Some would even take out several photos of their kids to show their passengers, and sometimes they would borrow photos from their friends as they didn't have kids of their own.

After talking to my second seating passengers about the comment card and they were leaving my table, I noticed one of my passengers talking to the dining room manager at the door. A few moments later, the manager approached me and asked how I explained the card. I told him and asked him, "Why, what was wrong?"

"Nothing, I hope," he said. But that gentleman was a travel writer, and he was curious why I was explaining the card. I didn't think he would write to the company, but I had to wait and see. It turns out he didn't.

That cruise I made what they called five stars. That meant all of my passengers—all twenty-four of them—gave me an excellent rating for both food and service. There were no complaints, so I got to keep my station for another cruise.

On that first cruise as a waiter, I also learned quickly was that death is unavoidable even at sea, and just like on land there are several forms of death, from suicides to murder, heart attacks, and other natural causes. When it's one's time to go, it can even happen on a cruise ship.

During my second week on board, I met a waiter, Kaya, from Turkey. He was in his late twenties and was tall with very dark hair and a mustache. He was quiet, reserved, and spoke very good English. He had worked on the ship for 10 years and gave me some good advice on how to survive on the ship, the best way to make money, move up, and deal with all of the politics, say nothing, and stay away from drugs and booze. He gave me a running start with a heads up on the competition.

One day we had arrived at Puerto Plata, in the Dominican Republic, and I decided to stay on the ship until I felt comfortable enough to go ashore. I knew this would only be true if I had someone to guide me.

We made three ports of call in one week. The first stop was Puerto Plata in the Dominican Republic, followed by San Juan, Puerto Rico, and the last stop was St. Thomas in the U.S. Virgin Islands. They would divide the waiters into three groups and each group would have a day off in each port. Without asking for it, I was given Puerto Plata. I didn't know any better, but I later found out that St. Thomas was the better choice and only the long-time waiters would have that privilege.

Kaya had told me he liked Puerto Plata as his day off because it was not so commercialized and a great way to escape from the pressure of the ship. It was also cheap; you could buy a beer for 50 cents, a sort-of meal for $2, and if you wanted a girl for the whole day, it was $20.

Later on, that night after the ship had left Puerto Plata, I found out that Kaya, only 28 years old, had died. He had rented a motorbike for the day and while turning a corner up a steep hill in the mountains, he crashed into a horse in the middle of the road. The man who owned the horse was so concerned about his horse, which had turned out to be just fine, nothing wrong with him. Meanwhile, he did not care to see if Kaya was okay. He felt his horse had more value than a human life, I found that out to be true later when I learned that Kaya was bleeding profusely and was in terrible shape. It was three hours later when Kaya arrived in the local hospital that they pronounced him DOA, dead on arrival. Kaya left behind a young wife and two kids. A memo went out that night to all crew on the ship that we were all banned from renting any motorbikes on the island from that day forward.

A couple of cruises later, I was running a station of sixteen passengers on each seating. At the start of another cruise, the restaurant manager, after giving out the stations, came to me with a very unusual request. He told me I had a family of eight at one of my round tables. The family included a mother, father, their two sons, as well as their wives, and a daughter and her husband. They were coming together from several parts of the United States.

The parents were traveling from California, the daughter was coming from New York, the two boys were from Nebraska and Colorado, and this was the first time the whole family would be all together in eight years. One thing they didn't know was that on the way from California, their father had a heart attack and died on the plane and when arriving in Miami their mother decided to continue with the cruise and had the body flown back to L.A. Their request was for me to always set the table for eight as if their father was there. It was a difficult first few days for me and the family. I could not be my cheery self and did not know how to speak to them, but I set an extra place, as they requested, at every meal. They would come to the dining room and frequently break out crying at the table. Their mother was very strong and held the family together for the whole cruise. After a couple of days, they opened up a bit and I could talk to them more. At the end of the cruise, they thanked me so much for everything and said that they felt their father was with them during the whole cruise.

I remember on another cruise an elderly couple were celebrating their 50th wedding anniversary; they arrived in the dining room dressed to the nines with big smiles on their faces. After a good meal of lobster and filet mignon, we brought their anniversary cake to the table. The other guests and a group of waiters gathered around the table and sang the anniversary song. As soon as it was over, the man grabbed his chest and collapsed at the table. The ship's doctor was called immediately, and a stretcher was brought, along with the nurse. They removed the man as quickly as possible and without disturbing the other passengers. Later that night, I found out that he'd had a massive heart attack and died an hour later in the ship's infirmary.

Similarly, one week, a couple in their late sixties, full of energy, signed up for all of the tours, determined to do it all and have a good time. One morning in Cozumel, the couple were booked on a short tour of the island. Cozumel is a small island off the coast of the Yucatan Peninsula of Mexico. One can see most of the island in a couple of hours. There is only one main road that goes around the whole island and then they drop you off in the village to do some shopping. It's funny how all of the tours on all of the stops always drop off at the local shops to entice you to spend more money.

When they finished their quick tour of the shops, they came back to the ship for a quick lunch, to change their clothes, and then they were off on another tour, a short walk down the pier where a dive boat was waiting to take a group of passengers a mile offshore to a coral reef diving site.

They boarded the small boat, and as they made their way to the reef, they were instructed about the workings of all of the equipment that they would wear on the dive. They were feeling very confident because this would not be the first time that they both would dive; they had done it on another cruise on the Mediterranean, off the coast of Greece.

As they both put on their fins and secured their tanks on their backs, the last thing was to purge the air with one or two pushes on a button on the mouthpiece, and then adjust their masks. Holding hands, they leaned backwards on the side of the boat and splashed into the turquoise waters. After coming up to the surface a couple of times, the next time his wife came to the top screaming, "My husband, my husband, he's on the bottom!" At the first scream, two professional divers dove overboard and a couple of minutes later they dragged the body onto the boat. They immediately tried CPR while the captain of the boat raced back to shore. When they arrived at the hospital, they pronounced the man dead. He had a heart attack while under the water.

There are many passengers who take cruises to improve their health. In fact, often their own doctors tell them to take a cruise. They say it will do a world of good. Yet it sometimes becomes the last cruise they ever take. With all of the excess eating and drinking, along with too much sun, and rushing around the stores on each island, it turns into too much for them, and their hearts then give up.

We carried several black body bags each cruise and would often use one or two per cruise. After the doctor pronounced them dead, he would put them into one bag and then the body was put into one of the refrigerators downstairs. The fridge they would use would often have cases of beer in the same room. In fact, I remember a good story when one of the waiters was told to go into the fridge to get a case of Heineken; he came out terrified when he found a dead body in there. When we arrived back in the States, home port, the coroner would board the ship to examine the body and then it would be removed from the ship after all of the paperwork was done by the captain and the ship's doctor.

Death happens in many ways, just like on land. We had several suicides, among both passengers and crew, and accidents resulting in death and murder. The ship is just like a small city and nowadays they are like large cities carrying up to 8,000 people.

I have known several cases where a passenger has gone missing. Later on, we found out that someone had seen them looking over the back deck late in the evening and they were never seen again. They apparently jumped overboard, and even if the ship's captain was alerted, there is a better chance of finding a needle in a haystack than finding a body at sea in the middle of the night in the warm waters of the Caribbean. One is more likely to be eaten by a shark than freeze to death from hypothermia like in the North Sea. I have been told one will not last over seven minutes in the North Sea if one falls in. A person's body will do all it can to keep the vital organs alive, from the heart to the brain and such, and close down the rest of the body one organ at a time. The last to go is the heart, followed by the brain.

On the other hand, a shark might let you live a little before devouring you. An old sailor once told me you shouldn't stare too long at the waves over the side of the ship, as it can hypnotize you and make you jump overboard, I don't know if this is true, but sometimes when I would go up on deck to relax, I would stand at the back of the ship and stare at the stars in the clear sky, and then I would look below at the waves crashing at the side of the ship. I would try to follow the wave that was created by the large propellers some 30 feet under the water until they would disappear into the darkness. You can get deeply involved in the motion. I found it very relaxing after a hard day's work.

Another way in which people fall overboard and some people may think it to be suicide is when some passengers and maybe crew have a few drinks too many and head up on deck to get some fresh air. There have been times when they have climbed up onto the rail and slipped and fallen overboard, never to be seen again.

I remember one Christmas morning we all got up around 6:00 a.m. like every other morning. We arrived at the restaurant and one of the head waiters checked us off on a big list. This was a ritual every morning to make sure all of us were up and ready for work.

That morning, just before we were about to open the doors to the guests, one of the waiters shouted how his busboy, Angelo, was missing. He hadn't shown up for work. The head waiter, along with another waiter, went down to his cabin to wake him up, but when they got to his cabin, he was not there. After searching a few other places, the head waiter called the bridge to report a crew member missing to the captain. The ship's staff immediately started a full search of the ship. The restaurant was opened and the guests were making their way to their tables unaware of what was happening down below while the search continued throughout the morning. They searched everywhere.

Later that morning, the ship's carpenter went to his storeroom and found Angelo, hanging from a pipe in the ceiling. He had a coarse rope around his neck and a small stool was upturned just inches from his feet. I saw the photos later that day. He had only been two months away from home and was very homesick. At only 22 years old, they later found a suicide letter in his locker. I can't imagine how his parents must have felt. That was the worst Christmas I can ever remember. I still remember it like it was yesterday, although it was 20 years ago. The guests soon found out, as did all of the crew members. It affected everyone that cruise and the mood that Christmas Day was very subdued.

Suicide is more common on cruise ships than one might think. People think of cruises as sailing on the open seas with the sun shining, visiting beautiful islands and beaches without a care in the world. They wonder why, under these conditions, anyone would contemplate suicide. The fact is that many passengers plan to leave this world long before they take the cruise and figure it makes for an easy way to call it a day. Crew members get lonely and miss their families. They have serious conflicts going on in their mind or certain circumstances arise and they can't deal with the stress any longer.

One such case was when a crew member was accused of raping a sixteen year old girl. One morning the young girl went to her parents, who had been looking for her all night and had half of the ship's officers looking for her. She was crying and saying that one of the crew had taken her to his room and forced her to have sex with him. The parents immediately demanded to see the captain. The girl's mother was hysterical; they were screaming at the captain to do something. The captain immediately called the ship's doctor to attend to the young girl and then assigned a few of his officers to investigate the report. After talking to the girl, it was not long before they identified the crew member. Upon interviewing him, his story was that the same girl was asking him all cruise to meet up with him and that the previous night she had a few too many drinks and wandered down to the crew area. When he saw her, he said he tried to send her back upstairs and somehow she ended up in his cabin and she forced herself on him. However it happened he should have known that she was only sixteen and that it would get him into a lot of trouble.

The investigation went on for a couple of days and he knew he was about to be arrested when the ship reached the next port of call. The night before we reached our destination, he committed suicide. He was found in his cabin with a rope around his neck hanging from a steel pipe from the ceiling.

Working on a cruise ship can be quite stressful for most of the crew and many of the crew have a different way of handling the stress. Besides suicide, some take drugs, some use alcohol, and some exercise in the gym. Others take it in stride.

One such person was Robert from Jamaica. He was a great person and a great waiter. He always had the highest ratings from his passengers and was the poster boy of the cruise line. There was even a large poster of him in the head office in which he was carrying a flaming baked Alaska on his head. It was the same photo I looked at the day I went to the office to find out if I was going to start work.

Robert had the biggest smile. He had worked for 10 years on the ship. In fact, he was one of the first waiters to join the new cruise line back in the early-70s. Robert seemed to handle all of the pressures of the job very well. He once told me he relied on God and his family to get through the rough days. He was a deeply religious person.

Robert had a beautiful wife of six years and two beautiful girls. Amy was six and Linda was four. I met his family several times when we would go to Ocho Rios (Spanish for eight rivers), a nice port in Jamaica where there is a waterfall to climb. It was used in the James Bond movie, *Thunderball,* with Sean Connery.

One day during dinner, Robert slipped and fell on the back crew staircase leading down from the kitchen. He hit his head badly. One of the other waiters found him and immediately called the ship's doctor to come. When the doctor arrived, he talked to Robert to make sure he was conscious. The doctor immediately asked two of the nurses to get a stretcher and he planned to bring Robert down to the ship's infirmary to check him over. However, the fall was so bad that he ended up in the hospital in Miami.

Several months later, he was back on board, working again. During his first dinner back, I noticed he was acting strangely. He was mixing up the orders and was very late coming out of the kitchen. This was not the professional waiter I knew from before. I went to the dining room manager, Roberto from Italy, to tell him how I thought something was wrong. After watching Robert work, he too said that Robert was not well enough to have already returned to his job, so he sent him to his room to rest. Later on, when one of his roommates went down to get a cigarette from the room, he came up to the restaurant hysterical saying that he thought Robert was dead. I ran downstairs to check on him, and when I entered the room, he was lying on his back, in his bunk. I told his roommate to call the doctor immediately. I then checked for air, checking his breathing. When I opened his mouth, I could see something blocking his airway. I put my finger into his mouth to move it, but when I pulled it out, it was his false teeth. I tried pushing down on his chest, but there was no sign of life. Roberto, the manager, heard what happened and he arrived to the room, asking if the doctor was called. We said yes; however, it had already been 20 minutes since we'd called. The doctor eventually arrived and just stood there, frozen, unsure what to do. It was only when he heard the captain coming to the room that he started pounding on Robert's chest.

We all knew it was too late. He was gone. Later on, after a hearing on board, the ship's doctor and nurse were both fired. Later that day, Robert's wife came on board to identify her husband's body and collect all of his belongings. I didn't know how she would explain this to their two young girls. The company paid for his body to be brought to his home in Jamaica, and for all of the funeral arrangements. Later that day, we found 14 empty bottles of Scotch whisky in his locker; the cause of death was that he choked to death while intoxicated. This was a man who never had an alcoholic drink in his life before his slip on the stairs. Even after 18 years, I can still see Robert's big smiling face and hope that the good Lord is looking after him and his family.

One friend of mine told me a story about a captain who was found dead in his cabin one morning after he didn't report to the bridge on our way back into the Miami Port. It was later on that I found out he had taken an overdose of painkillers and left a note to his wife saying he took his life. It was never proven, but supposedly he was deep into importing cocaine into the U.S. and tried to get out of a deal, but his contacts in Miami would not let him. They threatened him by saying if he quit, his wife and kid would be murdered in their sleep, so he eventually found a way out.

A similar case I remember hearing about involved a captain who was found floating in the Miami harbor. This was back in the late 1970s or early 1980s. After they recovered the body from the bay, they identified it as belonging to Captain Oloff, who was the captain of one of the largest cruise ships sailing out of Miami.

He went missing a couple of months earlier. It's believed, but has never been proven, that he also was heavily involved in the drug trade, and after several years, he decided it was time to get out. However, he found out how difficult it is to get out when he confronted his drug contact in Miami. It's believed that they had other plans, and they took care of him as only they knew how. Once you're in, you're in for life. There is no getting out, because you know too much.

Over the fifteen years I spent on the water, I also lost many friends to another killer—AIDS. AIDS does not discriminate. Many of my friends were gay; however, I knew many who were not who also died of the devastating disease. Very little was known back in the early 1980s when I started working for the cruise, but soon after, in the late 1980s and into the early 1990s, we began to understand what exactly AIDS was all about; however, by then, it was too late for many.

One great friend and countryman of mine from Ireland was Liam, a waiter. He was a young man who was about five foot six, had dark hair, was very skinny with a pale complexion, and had a great smile and a twinkle in his eye. He would light up a room. His life was taken by AIDS. What a person he was, and I can truly say I was privileged to have known him for the short time that I did. Liam was only 28-years-old when he died. He was a great entertainer, and he could, and did, perform in front of a large audience. He was a gifted comic and singer, and he even sang with the Irish duo, The Clancy Brothers, when they were on a cruise with us several years prior to his death.

Liam would help you get through the day if you were having a bad one, and when you felt low, he would lift you up. I remember one incident that brightened my day. It was 6:15 one morning, and we were at sea and getting ready for a busy breakfast. I woke up that morning not feeling my best, but I knew in about an hour, I would have to turn on my smile and get ready to greet my passengers.

During the days at sea, you could expect all or most passengers to show up, even though in reality they could continue to sleep as we would not be in any port that day, but they always felt, "Hey, I paid for this meal, so I will not miss it."

On this day, all of my passengers showed up—all twenty of them—at 7:00 a.m., half asleep. We would look around at the other waiters' stations, and if we saw that all of their passengers had shown up, we would shout BINGO (meaning they had a full house). Most of the guests would smile, but they didn't know what we really meant; it was our secret.

Before the passengers arrived, when we were getting our tables ready and setting all of the linens, china, etc., Liam arrived late, as usual. None of us spoke much that early in the morning, as we would save it for our guests, but I always greeted Liam, my fellow Irishman, with a warm, "Good morning, Liam, how do you feel today?" to which he replied, while stretching his arms in the air and letting out a big yawn, "Oh, I feel like a new man, but where would I find one this hour of the morning?" We all roared with laughter and that set the tone for the day, I will surely miss him. Without really knowing, he made our lives brighter.

***

The worst case of death I saw at sea happened one Friday night on our way back to Miami at the end of the cruise. There was a poker game going on in one of the crew bars. Although it was against company policy to have any gambling on board, many crew members, after getting their pay and tips on the last night of the cruise, found ways to lose their money before returning to Miami. The poker games would start around midnight and go on until daybreak. I know some waiters would stay up all night playing and lose all their money just in time to take a quick shower and go to work in the morning. These games usually took place in the crew bar or even in some cabins. It was not uncommon to have several games going on the same night in various parts of the ship, even in the Chinese laundry.

Usually one person would be on watch outside of the door for any officers who might pass, or for the night watch security who, if he saw any gambling going on, would call the bridge on his radio and everyone would be brought in front of the captain and usually fired the next day. This particular Friday night there were six players. Two were Filipino, from housekeeping, one was from Jamaica and worked as a cook, there was one bellman from Indonesia, and two waiters from Turkey. They were playing for about two hours when an argument erupted. The Jamaican cook was accusing one of the Filipino housekeepers of cheating.

The argument got heated and there was a lot of shouting back and forth. After the Jamaican threw his cards across the room and kicked the table, he stood up and walked out of the bar. Everyone continued to play, and about ten minutes later the Jamaican cook returned and walked right up to the table where they were still playing, and without a word pulled out a revolver from behind his back and pointed it about an inch from the Filipino's head and pulled the trigger. Blood splattered across the wall and he fell forward on the table—dead. The Jamaican ran out of the room and returned to his cabin. The bridge was informed and the staff captain and a couple of officers went to his room and found him sleeping. They woke him up and dragged him up to a small padded cell behind the bridge where he would spend the rest of the night locked up with an officer posted outside.

As the crime happened at sea and outside of the jurisdiction of the U.S., he was tried on board by the Norwegian authorities, as the ship was registered in Norway. He was convicted of first-degree murder and sentenced to life. He was then transported to a Norwegian prison where he is likely still living to this day.

The very next morning I was working in the dining room. Our ship was docked in Old San Juan, Puerto Rico. I heard several waiters running around saying, "Did you hear what happened to the shuttle? It exploded over the Atlantic Ocean." A group of us quickly ran down to our cabins and switched on our televisions. We were picking up a local station in San Juan. We stood there, shocked, as we watched the Challenger Space Shuttle take off from Cape Canaveral and explode after only 73 seconds into the flight. The explosion killed all seven astronauts on board. I can still see that image in my head all these years later.

There are three moments in history that I will always remember where I was, one being when President Kennedy was assassinated in 1963. I was a very young seven year old sitting on the floor watching it on our black and white TV. In Ireland, they gave us the day off of school to watch the funeral. The second moment was the Challenger disaster. And the third was the collapse of the twin towers in New York on September 11, 2001.

All of this happened on my first contract, which was supposed to be one year. However, after six months, I wanted to take a break and go home. I was dating a girl from Ireland and we had written to each other over the six months. I honestly was not sure if I wanted to stay on the ship, so I took a break and flew back to Ireland for six weeks. I had a good time at home. Everyone wanted to hear all of my stories and see all of the photos I took, especially of the islands. My girlfriend was great, and we took up where we left off six months earlier. I knew, though, that at the end of my six weeks, I would have to make a tough decision.

I had changed. The ship life will do that to you. At the end of my six weeks, I made the tough decision to go back to the ship. I felt it was the right choice to make, though I was leaving my girlfriend again and I would miss Ireland. I knew a long-distance relationship would be difficult and pretty much impossible; we wrote a couple of times after I went back, but sadly it didn't last.

CHAPTER 5

The Good, the Bad, and the Ugly

I returned to the same ship that I started on and got right back into the routine. I found it easier than I thought it would be. I quickly moved up my station size from sixteen to eighteen people, and then to the largest station in the center of the dining room with twenty passengers each seating. This meant a lot more money, as the center of the dining room was where the best passengers were seated. The dining room manager handpicked them himself, so he wanted the best waiters in his section. With a full station, you were guaranteed at least eight hundred dollars per week. This was good money back in the early 1980s.

Along with one's station and working around fourteen hours per day, everyone had a side job. I had several over the years, from being in charge of all of the uniforms that each waiter and busboy would wear every day, to collection of all of the uniforms at the end of each shift. There were side jobs like wake-up man, where you would have to get up earlier than everyone else and go around to all of the cabins to wake everyone. During this time when I first returned to the ship, I was in charge of all of the linen and napkins, issuing every waiter his allotment of napkins for each day. I would then count them every month for inventory. I had help from a couple of other waiters who would go to the laundry to collect the correct linens each day.

One night one of the waiters went to the laundry to pick up the linen for the next day when he heard a strange rustling sound over in one corner he ran out of the laundry scared and ran all the way up to the dining room several decks above, when he approached me he could hardly speak, he was white as a sheet, I asked him to slow down and tell me what happened, he explained to me he heard a sound in the laundry room, so I followed him back down to see what he was talking about. As we approached a large pile of dirty sheets in the corner of the laundry it started to move, a moment later a body appeared from under the pile, he was as scared as we were, it turned out that he was a stowaway that got on board in Jamaica and had planned to hide out until we would reach Miami and then find someway to exit the ship there. I Made a phone call to the bridge and he was taken into custody until we reached back to Jamica the following week and was taken off the ship.

After a couple of months doing this side job, I noticed we were losing a lot of napkins—especially white ones. I watched carefully and noticed that we were losing about one hundred napkins per cruise. I began counting the white napkins each day, and I noticed the napkins missing after we left Jamaica. I mentioned this to the food and beverage manager who was concerned because he was the person who had to sign a requisition for linen from Miami, and his bonus was built into making sure the inventory was correct and his costs were in line, so he would not believe me. He told me, "I don't believe that. You must be counting them wrong."

One day while we were docked in Montego Bay, I was working during lunch in the dining room when the food and beverage manager came running over to me saying, "Harry, you were right, you were right." He was out of breath when he reached me, and he again said, "You were right. We stopped a cleaner going off the ship with a large bag and searched it. We found a bundle of napkins, silverware, and ashtrays in his bag. He was selling them to a local restaurant in town that's owned by his cousin."

They fired the crew member in question on the spot. They also beefed up security at every port after that.

During my second contract, I met many passengers from all parts of America and from different backgrounds. Some were very nice, and some were not. In any service industry, you are bound to find difficult customers, and there is no exception in the cruise industry.

One cruise; Italian Night, I was working as a waiter and had a station at the far end of the restaurant the furthest away from the kitchen. I was a bit behind so I started to speed up a bit, I was carrying a trey of sixteen plates of pasta from the kitchen and decided to take a short cut though the buffet line which had a marble floor, as I passed I stepped on something slippery and all I can remember was sliding on the floor as my trey flew into the air and the plates went flying, as I got up I looked over at a table of six people all dressed up to the nineties and they were pulling spaghetti out of there hair and cloths. The head waiter Serge came to my rescue, he first asked me if I was all right, then he said go back to the kitchen and get your order again and I will take care of this table. I returned to the kitchen a bit shaken and collected my food again and proceeded to my station to serve all the meals ,meanwhile the guests that had all the pasta over them had to go to there rooms, take a shower, change cloths and return to the dining room to eat, after I was finished I went over to apologize to them they were more concerned about me and had a good laugh about the whole thing and even took pictures of me, I was lucky and lucky I had a great head waiter to act quickly and take care of a bad situation, thank you Serge.

There are tough customers and there are tougher ones yet. During my time on board, it usually started before they boarded the ship, maybe on the plane that was delayed for two hours while they were getting to the ship, or maybe with the taxi driver who was rude and wouldn't help them with their luggage. Sometimes a porter dragged their cases on the ground. In any case, when they arrived on board tired and hungry, they tended to already be upset and ready to argue with anyone. It was our job to convince them they could leave all of their troubles behind and that it would be smooth sailing from that point forward; however, that was not always the case. I remember one couple who were screaming at the chief purser, because their luggage did not reach their cabin. The last time they saw their luggage was back in L.A. before they boarded the plane. The chief purser was trying to convince them that there were still three hours before the ship would sail and that he would check out what had happened to their luggage. It turned out that the couple were in the wrong room and their luggage was in their room waiting for them for the last two hours. They were very embarrassed, and after apologizing to the chief purser, they became good friends throughout the whole cruise. In fact, they kept in touch for years, and when the chief purser was getting married, he invited them to his wedding.

Over the course of my 14 years on many cruise ships, I came across many difficult passengers, but none so difficult as a couple who sailed every Christmas cruise. They complained about everything from the moment they stepped on board, so much so that every crew member knew them. They would book the cheapest cabin, and then the moment they came on board, they would complain that the room was too small, hoping to get a free upgrade. They complained about their seating arrangements for dinner so they could get a table near the captain's table. They would complain about the food, the room service, and, well, you get the picture.

I remember their last cruise. It was Christmas Eve and the captain's dinner. The captain would give a cocktail party before dinner and introduce his officers to the passengers. They would pass around drinks and hors d'oeuvres, then everyone—including the captain—would have dinner in the dining room. On every captain's dinner night, we poured free champagne for all of our guests. When this couple received their champagne, they said to me, "Can't the Captain provide better champagne than this? This tastes like crap." At that moment, the gentleman stood up from his chair, walked over to the captain's table, and poured the glass of champagne on the table in front of the captain and his guests. He said to the captain, "I don't care for your choice of champagne," then walked back to his table. The captain, trying not to upset his guests' dinner, just smiled and said nothing except to apologize to his guests for the interruption.

After the captain and hotel manager complained to the head office, they sent the couple a letter from the company to say they would not be permitted to cruise with our cruise line ever again. In essence, we fired the guests. In this case the guest was not always right.

During another cruise, a couple came up to the Purser's Office on the last night of the cruise to complain that someone had stolen a wedding ring from their cabin. They insisted it was their cabin steward. After the hotel manager and staff captain did an investigation, they could not find the ring, yet the couple still accused their cabin steward of having stolen it.

After several interviews with Juan, the cabin steward in question, they could not find any reason to find him guilty; however, the company fired him in front of the guests. He was handcuffed by the Immigration authorities and taken to the Miami International Airport and deported to his country of Honduras. The couple left the ship the same morning without the ring and vowed never to return to the ship or company again.

The very next cruise, the new cabin steward was cleaning the same room when he moved the bed to tuck in the blankets. The ring fell to the floor.

He brought the ring to the hotel manager who called the office to notify the couple that they had found the ring; they did not even apologize for getting their cabin steward in trouble and consequently fired and deported.

The company called Juan in Honduras and offered him his job back, to which he replied, "I worked for you for 15 years and if you didn't trust me to be an honest person all that time and stand up for me, I don't want to be a part of your company."

I later learned that Juan spent the rest of his life with his family in Honduras and never returned to any ship; though he sometimes regrets not going back. He felt good about his decision.

I remember one night in the dining room, I was a head waiter and doing my rounds checking each table to see that everyone was taken care of, when I noticed a table that looked like something was wrong. I asked the table's waiter what was wrong, and he told me it was the second night of the cruise and the people were never happy with anything he brought them. I told him I would see what I could do to help. As I approached the table of six, consisting of three couples by the window, I was watching their body language and could see immediately that the couple—especially the woman on the end of the table—did not look happy. When I got to the table, I asked if there was anything I could do to help. The lady picked up the edge of her plate and flipped the plate over, making it crash on the table, spilling her food. She said, "This food tasted like shit."

At that moment, I could feel the blood rushing to my head. In all my years working on cruise ships, I had never lost my temper with a guest; however, this time I could feel my blood starting to boil, and I replied, "Madam, we don't serve shit in this restaurant." I then walked away because I was afraid of saying too much. I walked down a couple of tables and when I looked back in their direction, I saw her husband look at me. With his finger, he called me back to their table. I approached again, wanting to let them know I was not scared—although I was. I kept thinking how this would be my last cruise since I would probably get fired for what was about to happen.

When I arrived at the table, the lady would not look at me, but her husband said, "Well, are you going to tell him or not, because I sure am not." She looked up at me and said, "I apologize. I should not have said that to you." At that moment, I knew I had them in the palm of my hand for the rest of the cruise.

I replied, "May I take this away for you and find you something you would like? I hear the chicken is excellent."

She said, "That sounds great, if you don't mind."

"No trouble at all. I will be back in a moment with your chicken."

After that first night, everything was smooth sailing. When they were leaving the ship on Saturday, they said it was the best cruise that they had ever taken and would look forward to seeing me the next year.

***

Employees can be difficult too. One night I was working the midnight buffet. It was the Gala Buffet and one of my jobs was to speak on the microphone about the buffet. I had done this many times before, and I was about halfway through the speech when the hotel manager staggered into the dining room. He was a man in his sixties wearing a black suit that was not buttoned up correctly, and he had some stains on his shirt where it looked like some of his dinner missed his mouth. We called him Johnnie Walker, after the whiskey, since he drank a bottle of Johnnie Walker Black every day and was never sober. This night was no exception. He staggered over to me and, with a slur in his voice, he told me I was not speaking well enough to the guests. He irritated me so much that I put the microphone down and walked away from him. He called me back and said if I walked away from him, he would see that I was fired, but I kept walking away and went to my room.

The next morning, the food and beverage manager asked me what happened. I told him the story and that I do not respect someone who is drunk on duty who will speak to me like that, even if it is the hotel manager. He said not to worry, that I wouldn't lose my job. In fact, the hotel manager did not even remember what happened that night. I feel to this day that they were afraid that I would have reported his behavior to the office ashore, and that he is the one who would have been fired. A couple of days later, the same hotel manager was transferred to another ship as a result of what had happened.

***

The captain has all of the responsibilities of running the ship, making sure the passengers are being cared for, that the crew is happy, and to play the role of policeman, judge, and jury. It's a tough job, and some captains literally take the law into their own hands. I remember one such captain; he had a complex about being short. He was only five feet, six inches, but he acted like he was ten feet tall. He loved to order everyone around, shouting and demanding that everything was to be done his way, without question.

One day we worked 14 hours straight because the weather was so bad, and we didn't make it to our first stop since we had to ride out the storm. Everyone was exhausted. After all, it's twice as tiring when trying to use leg muscles to balance while walking around the restaurant for hours, not to mention the night before none of us got much sleep because of the rough weather.

The captain decided to hold an inspection at the end of the day, He came into the restaurant and after an hour of checking every detail with a couple of his officers—white gloves and all—he decided the place was not up to speck, and he informed the restaurant manager that he would be back in the morning at 5:00 a.m. to re-inspect the restaurant all over again before the first passenger arrived for breakfast. All of the waiters were burned out and the fact that they would only get a couple of hours rest before the re-inspection made everyone very upset.

The message got back to the captain, so the next night he sent down ten cases of beer to the restaurant for all of the waiters to have with their dinner. However, everyone decided not to have a beer in protest, and the beer was returned to the captain. He was furious. He called the restaurant manager to assemble everyone in the restaurant for a meeting. When everyone was in the room, the captain arrived with one of his officers, and he spoke about how he had all of this responsibility and pressure as a captain and he was just doing his job. He then asked whose idea it was not to accept the beer.

For a moment, no one spoke. Then a waiter named Joe put up his hand and said it was his idea. The Captain told him to stand up and give his name. "Joe Brosnan," he replied.

The officer standing beside the captain started writing in a small book he was carrying. "So, Joe," the captain asked, "Why did you not accept the beer I sent to all of you?"

Joe said, "Because we all felt that you were giving us unnecessary stress and it was a protest against your actions." The captain said nothing for about two minutes, and then asked everyone who felt the same way to raise their hands. No one did.

The next day we arrived at our home port of Miami. Joe got a note from shoreside. When he opened it, he had five minutes to pack his bags and go through Immigration; he was out of a job.

***

I remember a couple once that no matter what we did, they were never happy; from the moment they stepped on board they found something to complain about. The captain, the hotel manager, the cruise director, and the restaurant manager all had problems with them. The couple complained about the location of their cabin and tried to get an upgrade; however, the ship was full and there were no empty cabins. They complained about the food in the dining room; it was too hot or too cold or not spicy enough for them. They complained about the shows, saying the singers and dancers were not professional. They complained to the captain about not staying longer in port even when the captain explained to them that in order to make the next port of call, the ship had to be on a strict schedule. By the end of the cruise, all of the staff were fed up with them and couldn't wait until they would leave. When the ship docked in Miami on the last day of the cruise, the hotel manager went to meet the Customs officer. Every time when the ship arrived in home port, one of their routines was to have a cup of coffee up on the veranda deck together.

It was during this time that the Customs officer would ask the hotel manager if there was anything suspicious that might have being going on during the cruise, to which the hotel manager replied, "No, nothing unusual for this cruise, however there is something else."

"And what was that?" the Customs officer asked.

"We had the worst passengers I've met in a long time."

"Exactly what do you mean?" asked the officer.

After the hotel manager explained all of the problems that they caused, the Customs officer asked the passengers' names. He then wrote them down in a small black book he was carrying.

"Don't worry," he said as he put the black book back in his top pocket and closed the flap. "I have an idea that may make them think twice about doing that again." The hotel manager looked confused, as he did not know where the Customs officer was going with his thinking.

It wasn't until later on that he found out that the Customs officer had arranged for the couple to be pulled aside after they had disembarked the ship. He later told us that the couple then then had every bag and case searched and it was arranged for them to be detained for almost two hours. Needless to say, they missed their flight and had to wait three more hours at the airport for another flight. When I told the rest of the crew what happened to them, everyone felt a little bit of sweet revenge. Justice had been served.

***

Another time, we had just set off from Miami for a two-week cruise; we opened the restaurant doors for the first seating dinner when I noticed three older gentlemen sitting outside. They looked like they were in their eighties and were dressed in very old, ragged suits and were badly shaven, along with having a bad odor coming from them. I assumed they were waiting for someone, so when I asked them are they on the first or second seating, they didn't respond. Later that night, when I opened the doors for the second seating and after everyone entered the room, I saw the three men still sitting outside. I asked them again if they were coming in to eat. One gentleman looked up at me and said how they didn't have any money and couldn't afford to eat. I told them that it was all included on the cruise, so I found them seats.

When the food came, they ate it like they hadn't eaten in a week. Later on, I notified the hotel manager, and he checked if there was anyone traveling with them. It turned out that they were from a nursing home that was closed for two weeks' worth of renovations, and the staff did not find any next of kin to take in the three men while the home was closed so they took some of their savings and dropped them off at the cruise terminal with their tickets. The home was later fined and some of the staff were fired.

Despite this, the three gentlemen had a great time. The ship's doctor looked them over and the nurse cleaned them up and took care of them for the two weeks.

They ate every day in the restaurant, and even the other guests would come by and chat with them from time to time. Two of the three men were suffering from Alzheimer's, a devastating disease that would take my dad many years later.

***

It would not be fair just to talk about the difficult passengers without telling about some of the nicer guests. There are plenty of pleasant people who take cruises.

There was a nice young couple I met on my first cruise. They were on their honeymoon and I was their busboy. Since it was the first cruise for the both of us, we had something in common.

I remember having great chats about Ireland and how they wanted to visit someday. I was nervous on my first cruise trying to learn everything, but they made me feel at ease. And when the cruise was over and we said our goodbyes, little did we know our paths would kind of cross again many years later.

Twelve years later, a couple was checking into a hotel where my wife, Meridith, was working at the front desk. As they were checking in, Meridith asked them if they were on vacation or on business when they said they were going on a cruise in the morning to celebrate an Anniversary . Meridith said, "Oh, my husband used to work on a cruise ship." She then produced a photo of me and when the couple looked at my photo they were astonished and couldn't believe their eyes. They said, "That's Harry, he was our busboy twelve years ago when we were on our honeymoon and I believe it was his first cruise, too. You must tell Harry that we are going on this cruise tomorrow with our two nine-year-old twin daughters to celebrate our twelfth anniversary." It amazes me how small the world really is, and how often we realize it.

Back in the early 1980s, it was still considered a luxury to take a cruise. It was not until later that Carnival Cruise Line started offering cruises at a cheap price to catch another part of the market, and at that point, all of the other cruise lines followed.

Most of our passengers back then who took cruises every year were considered rich, or they saved up for years just to take a cruise.

I remember one such cruise when I was a waiter, and I had a table of six by the window. There were three couples, and on the first night out, each couple was introducing each other and the usual chit chat started. They would ask where everyone was from, if they had any children, etc. After a few days into the cruise, it was easy to tell that one couple had done a lot of traveling and had taken several cruises. The other couple had traveled also, but they did not mention it as much, while the last couple didn't say anything, and it was apparent that they had little in common with the first couple who at every meal would talk about all of their trips and were comparing all of their other cruises with the one they were presently taking. They bragged a lot about their trips to Europe.

At the end of the cruise it was customary to tip the waiter around twenty-eight dollars per couple for the week's cruise, so at the end of the cruise I received three envelopes from that table. One envelope was from the couple that had taken all of the trips. It had twenty dollars in it. The second couple had thirty dollars inside, and the couple that had saved up all of their money for this once in a lifetime trip left a note in the envelope. I opened it up to read it, and it said, "Harry, you made our trip, we will never forget the experience and the way you took care of us. We felt like royalty. We are sorry that we don't have as much money as the other guests at your table. We would love to give you more."

After reading the letter, I took out a fifty-dollar note from the same envelope.

As my mother always told me, "Never judge a book by its cover."

I will always remember that couple and learned a great lesson from them. I also often wondered if they ever got to take another cruise.

There was the couple that came on the same two week Christmas cruise every year and were always excited to see the same staff each year. They always asked for the same waiter and busboy and cabin steward to take care of them. They traveled with their daughter who was about eight-years-old the first year we met, and when we would get to port, they brought me on some of their shore trips; we knew them so well that they were like family. Every year we would see their daughter grow up. On Christmas morning, when they came for breakfast, they would have a Christmas present for me and my busboy and we would all open our presents together at the table. They knew we were feeling sad not being home with our own families, so they wanted to make sure we had a second family that we all could share the holidays with while working.

There was one couple who requested to sit at a table for two on their own because the wife had been stricken with a terrible case of skin cancer. Half of her face was eaten away with the cancer. It was so bad she had to have all of her food ground up in a food processor so she could drink it with a straw; she had no lips and looked like half her face was a skeleton. I was their waiter, and to be honest, the way she looked scared me. I did not know how to handle the situation, and most of the other waiters said they were glad it was me as they didn't know how to handle it either.

I got to know the couple over the week and although I felt very sorry for them—especially the husband—I realized they were a couple that was having a tough time but had a good life as well. They were doing the best they could under the circumstances. I admired the husband who would stick by his wife during this time and realized that their love for each other was stronger than anything else.

***

When I had worked on the ship for two years, there was great excitement in the dining room because the captain's waiter was leaving and everyone was wondering who would be the new captain's waiter. There were even bets going around about it. It was a tie between Carlos, a waiter from Spain, and myself; I didn't think I had a chance, but half of the dining room did.

To my surprise, the very next cruise they announced me as the captain's waiter.

CHAPTER 6

The Captain's Table

It was a big deal being the captain's waiter. It was like being the number one waiter on the ship; I was in charge of the captain when he came to the dining room.

There was a large empty table in the center of the dining room that was always kept available for the captain. Normally he came down for dinner two or three times per cruise. Most of the waiters came over to me to shake my hand and congratulate me on my new position. I had worked beside the last captain's waiter—Francisco from Italy—and watching him, I learned much about how to take care of not only the captain, but also his guests. The pace was a little slower than a regular table and I always waited for the captain to arrive before handing out the menus.

One of the biggest questions I and many waiters were asked each cruise was, "How do you get invited to the captain's table?"

We were never really allowed to tell any guest how it worked, but I will share the guarded secret with you.

At the beginning of each cruise, they would send a list from the main office to the dining room manager with the names of passengers whom they would like to have invited to join the captain at his table. It was called the VIP list.

Some names on the list could be celebrities from various fields, some major businesspeople, others could be friends of the owners, some could be passengers who had sailed with the cruise line many times, and there were always a couple of young, single ladies.

The captain never came down for dinner the first night as he was usually on the bridge, which served as the control and steering room at the top front of the ship. After a long day, he would have something sent up to his cabin to eat. The next morning, the dining room manager would have a meeting with the captain, and they would go over the VIP list. The captain would often have a copy of the same list. He would get it in a large brown envelope with other official papers from the main office. They would both decide together whom to invite to the table; however, the captain had the final say about whom he wanted at his table. Often he would see some passengers he knew from another cruise, or perhaps he would see a couple of single girls in the disco the night before and wanted them at his table.

If the dining room manager wanted to get on well with the captain, he would always have two beautiful women to sit on each side of the captain at dinner. This always made the captain happy. They were usually in their mid-twenties, about half the age of the captain. During dinner, I would often observe the captain put his hands on each of their legs. When the photographer would come around the dining room, he always took a photo of the captain's table, but none of the other guests at the table were aware what was going on, as he would do it under the tablecloth. The women had these big smiles on their faces. It's amazing what a uniform with gold bars on the shoulders will do.

For those who want to sit at the captain's table, try writing to the cruise line several weeks before and give them a great story so the letter stands out from the rest. Never go up to the dining room manager and ask him outright or try to shove some money into his hand. This will never work. Believe me. I've seen it all.

On my first cruise as the captain's waiter, I was a little nervous. There were four couples and two single ladies at the table. They were all sent invitations to their cabins in the afternoon with notes stating that they should meet the dining room manager at the end of the captain's cocktail party that evening. The dining room manager would bring them down to the dining room and seat them around the table, leaving an open seat for the captain. Then, he would collect the captain when all of the guests were already seated. The captain would be introduced by the dining room manager to the guests, and then the captain would sit down, and he would already know their names as he greeted them around the table. Some captains walked around the table and shook everyone's hands before sitting down themselves.

After the introductions, I would introduce myself and hand out the menus. Later on, as the captain got to know me better, he would often introduce me to his guests. I could see the guests were more nervous than I was about the seating arrangement. After a couple of cruises, I would talk to the guests before the captain would arrive so I could help break the ice and make them feel at ease. This was always better for the captain, too, and I know he appreciated it.

After I took the orders and went to get the appetizers, I returned to my station and noticed the dining manager standing beside the captain. The captain looked upset, and I immediately wondered if I had done something wrong. The captain then excused himself and left the table. His white jacket was covered with something red all down one side. I asked the dining room manager what had happened; he told me a new waiter carrying a tray of tomato soup passed by the table and one soup slipped off of his tray and fell on the captain's shoulder, spilling all of the hot soup down the captain's uniform. The captain went to his room to change and planned to return to the table. As a result, I had to slow down the service until he returned.

Ten minutes later, the captain returned and sat down with a new shirt and new jacket. I then went to the kitchen to get the main course.

The nice thing about being the captain's waiter was that no matter when I got to the kitchen, I would automatically move to the front of the line and the executive chef would serve me himself with the food for the captain's table.

As I returned to the dining room, the captain was missing again. I asked the guests what had happened and they told me that the same waiter passed by the table again and dropped a plate of spaghetti on the captain. The Captain was so upset he refused to come down to the dining room the rest of the cruise. He believed the waiter had it in for him. Subsequently, the waiter was transferred to another ship at the end of the cruise.

The captain would usually get lucky with one of the single women at his table. He could be seen in the disco later that night and often I would have to bring some food to the captain's room, and I would see a girl sitting on his bed.

I remember years later when I was the dining room manager. One captain called me to his room the morning we arrived in our home port. He had a young lady in his cabin. I had seen her many times on several cruises and she always sat next to the captain at his table. He whispered to me, "Harry, I need to get rid of her. My wife is waiting to board the ship. Please go to the terminal and slowly escort my wife on board. Tell her I have the coast guard with me on the bridge and I will be with her soon."

When the captain asked for something to be done, it was never appropriate to say no, nor should it have ever been questioned, so off I went to walk down the gangway. I could see the captain's wife standing at the bottom, waiting to board. She smiled at me as I approached her and said, "Harry, what's up? They won't let me on board yet."

I said, "It won't be long."

I was about to tell her that the captain was busy on the bridge, but when I turned around, I could see the other woman at the top of the gangway. I looked at the captain's wife and said, "Everything is fine now; you can come on board. I will escort you to the captain's quarters."

We climbed the gangway and halfway up, we passed the other woman on the way down. As we passed, she stopped and said, "Harry, thank you for a great cruise," and "I will see you again soon." The captain's wife looked at me and smiled. She thought I had spent the cruise with the woman. I just smiled back.

***

All of the captains would have signs for me to let me know if they were not comfortable at the table and wanted to speed up the service, or sometimes slow down if they were having a good time and wanted to stay longer. They would let me know if they had to leave the table quickly, and I would step in and tell the captain they needed him on the bridge. At that point, he would excuse himself, thank everyone, and leave. There were several cruises during which the captain was not too happy with his guests, and he would look over to me and nod. That was my signal to move in and tell him within earshot of the guests that they needed him on the bridge.

Being the captain's waiter had its perks. I remember arriving on board late one day. This usually was followed by a trip to the captain's quarters for a severe warning, but when the captain found it was his personal waiter, nothing happened to me.

***

I started a hobby when I was on board collecting money (notes) from all around the world. It started when I was working as a waiter with a busboy from Yugoslavia. His name was Slavko, and I asked him if he had any money from Yugoslavia, and I offered him a couple of dollars for it, but he said no. One afternoon, I was showing a couple of waiters my collection when the captain walked through the dining room. He came over to us and asked me what we were all looking at, so I showed him my collection. I had over thirty countries by then. The captain asked me if I had any Norwegian money and I said no, so he said, "I will go home next week and bring back some for you."

I said, "Thanks, Captain, I look forward to that," thinking he wouldn't remember.

However, six weeks later, the captain returned. The first night he came to dinner he handed me the money. I still have that collection today, twenty years later.

***

One cruise I will never forget happened when I was still the captain's waiter. We had some royals at the captain's table all week.

Several weeks before they arrived, I was chosen to be the waiter for a lord and lady from England. They were a very high-profile couple. I was checked out by the FBI, and several other officials checked my whole background. I remember the day they came on board, security was on high alert, and snipers were strategically placed on the roofs of the pier terminal. As I was the captain's waiter, I got to meet them the first night for dinner; they arrived in the dining room after all of the other guests were seated, and as they approached the table, the captain stood up to shake their hands as I pulled out their chairs. They were a delightful couple and spoke with posh English accents. Except for the usual greeting of "Good evening, Your Ladyship and Lordship," I didn't speak to them unless they spoke to me first.

No one else could approach the table, and even though there were several security scattered through the dining room—men dressed in black suits wearing earpieces—I was instructed to watch for anyone who might try to approach the table. I would step in if this happened and say to please respect their privacy and not go any further. If anyone got too close, several of the black suits would be seen quickly rising from their tables and rushing towards the captain's table. All of the other waiters were very jealous because they expected I would get a huge tip. I kept telling them that royalty, and especially English royalty, were not used to tipping and that I expected little.

On the last night of the cruise, when it was customary to hand out the tipping envelopes, I was saying goodbye to His Lord and Ladyship when they handed me a large envelope with beautifully handwritten words that read "Thank you, Harry" on the front and a red waxed seal on the back. I waited until everyone had left the room and all of the other waiters rushed over to me.

"Come on, open it. We want to see what they gave you," they said to me. As I opened the envelope carefully and some of the hard wax dropped to the floor, I pulled out a crisp colored New Jamaican five-dollar bill. One American dollar was worth eight Jamaican Dollars. So, it was worth about eighty cents for a week of service. Everyone was shocked, except me. I told them again that royalty were not accustomed to tipping, and I really expected nothing. Although, nothing would have been better that what I got.

Six months later, the dining room manager, Rubin from Spain, a tall, slim man with brown hair, who was a soft spoken man, approached me. He had the respect of every waiter in the dining room, including me. He told me he was going over to Finland to pick up the new ship and that he wanted me to be the first waiter to be with him on the new ship. He said he would send for me in a couple of weeks. I was just to wait to hear from him, and the office would arrange everything, I was so excited and thanked him.

For the next couple of weeks, I couldn't wait to hear from him. Before long, he called me to say, "Sorry, Harry, you will not be coming to the new ship with me. The office has another plan for you." He added, "But don't worry. It will be better for you. I can't tell you what it is, but you won't be disappointed."

After I hung up, I felt let down, and wondered what could be better than starting on a brand new ship.

Two weeks later, I was called over to the office and Eric, the personnel manager whom I had worked with previously when he was a waiter, handed me two uniforms for a head waiter and said, "Congratulations. Tonight when the ships sails, you will be a head waiter." I shook his hand and walked back to the ship, excited for my new adventure.

CHAPTER 7

Watch the Ratings

I put on my new uniform and headed up to the dining room where I met with Roberto, the dining room manager from Italy. He was an unusually tall man who was slightly bald with a bushy mustache. He congratulated me and told me what my principal duties would be. He said this was a big change as I was on the management team as a result of the promotion, and I would therefore have more responsibilities; he explained to me there were four head waiters on the ship, including me, and that I would be responsible for a quarter of the dining room. This covered about three hundred passengers, twelve waiters, and eight busboys.

My first night, I introduced myself with each waiter and busboy to every table. Then I would help each waiter clear their tables in between each course, as well as check in the kitchen to make sure they were not delayed getting their food. At the end of service, I would go by each table again to wish them a good night. I made it a point of visiting each table three times every meal. At the end of each cruise,

I could see the difference in my envelopes. I remember the other head waiters were a lot older than I was and were looking at my pockets full of envelopes with envy. My other responsibilities were to help each waiter to make the ratings by evaluating each table and advising him on how to talk to his passengers. Sometimes it was better for the busboy to speak, especially if it was clear that the passengers were enjoying their busboy more than their waiter.

The way all cruise ship companies operate to provide outstanding service on board is with a rating system. The person who started this idea was a genius. Every department and every person on board is rated at the end of the cruise by each passenger. The way most systems work is a comment card is handed out to each passenger on the last night of the cruise along with the tipping envelopes. The card is divided up into each department like the cruise director, staff, food, and dining room service, housekeeping, bar, etc. Then each department is rated from 1, meaning poor service, to 5, meaning excellent service. By adding one's name, room number, and table number, the company can tell who each passenger's server is in the restaurant as well as the name of their cabin steward.

People's jobs and lives depended on those ratings. One bad rating, a slip of the pen, or a critical comment might mean being sent home, never to return, while an excellent rating ensured a job for the following week. The system worked so well for the cruise line; however, like any system, it had its flaws.

The first company I worked for was a concession. They provided all of the staff, along with food and beverages for the cruise line. In turn, the cruise line paid them a fee based on the number of passengers who sailed each cruise. This was another big reason for the ratings, as the cruise line would add one very important clause to the contract: "If the food and beverage ratings fell below a certain number, the cruise line would deduct a large percentage of payment to the food company." If over the year it was under another number, they would not sign a new contract for the following year. It's no wonder based on all of this information how the crew always seemed to be smiling and being so friendly. After all, their livelihoods were literally in the hands of their passengers.

As the cruise lines added more ships, there was always competition between each ship to come in with the highest ratings. The food company also offered bonuses to the food and beverage managers, as well as the restaurant managers when they would reach a certain number and beat the other ships. It was in the best interest of the food company to offer these incentives so they would be guaranteed a new contract at the end of each year. Of course, along with this and the heightened pressure comes cheating. The way it works is that when each passenger fills out the comment card, they drop it into a locked box, usually placed by the Purser's Office. The boxes would be taken off of the ship, brought to the cruise line office, then sorted through a machine to count the checkmarks. They were soon read by a group of people who worked for the cruise line, and the comments were printed out by room number, so by the time the ship was ready to sail, the final ratings and comments were sent back on board. The restaurant manager would then use this score to assign all of the stations for the next cruise. A bad or low rating with no bad comments would mean a small station and thus less tips that cruise. If this happened, a good waiter could lose two to five hundred dollars for the following cruise. A good or excellent rating would ensure a larger station and thus another two to five hundred extra the following cruise. A restaurant manager could be demoted or lose his job just for a low overall rating in one cruise, and sometimes just a cruise with bad weather could make it so many passengers wrote bad ratings. With all of this at stake, it makes sense how everyone was looking for ways to cheat the system.

One such case I remember was when one of the restaurant managers paid one engineer a reported $5000 to make a copy of the keys that locked the boxes. During the night, he and one of the head waiters sneaked down to the Purser's Office. After making sure no one was following them, they took the two boxes to their cabins, opened up the boxes, dumped all of the cards onto the floor in the cabin, then quickly replaced the locks and put the boxes back down by the Purser's Office again. When they returned to the cabin they checked each comment card to make sure there were no bad comments or that nobody had checked off a poor or fair on the card for the restaurant.

If they found any like this, they would simply destroy them. Sometimes they would add more comment cards themselves to help the ratings. This process took them about three hours every cruise. They would then go back and pick up the boxes, return to the cabin and put back all of the good cards, and return the boxes to the Purser's Office where they would be picked up after the ship docked. Sometimes they were just returning the boxes minutes before the ship was set to dock, cutting it very close.

This went on for several cruises until one night when they were heading to their cabin with the two boxes, they thought someone was following behind them, and they both turned their heads and looked back along the long corridor but saw no one. After they had opened the boxes and poured all twelve hundred cards onto the floor, the cabin door busted open. There, standing in the doorway, was the hotel manager, along with the captain. They had been caught, and both of them were fired and sent home the next day. After that, the boxes were moved to a location where they were watched by one officer, and the boxes were only put out until midnight, then moved to the hotel manager's office, where they remained until 6:00 a.m. They were eventually put back at the Purser's Office for passengers who missed putting them in the night before.

The next cruise, a new restaurant manager and head waiter were desperately looking for an alternative way to beat the system.

At the beginning of each cruise, the dining room manager would have a meeting with all the dining room staff. He would call out all of the waiters who made five stars, from the previous cruise, meaning they had a perfect rating from all of their passengers. I remember on one occasion there was a great waiter named Jesus from Spain. He always made five stars, but on this occasion he only made four stars. The dining room manager, Roberto from Italy, asked Jesus in front of all of the other waiters: "Jesus, what happened last cruise that you only made four stars instead of your usual five stars?"

Jesus replied, *"I'm only Jesus, not God."* Everyone, including Roberto, roared with laughter.

We had a problem when every passenger received a comment card and more and more families were traveling. This meant more kids would fill out those cards, and, of course, they were not aware how important they were, and how with one stroke of a pen they could destroy a person's career. in this case the pen can be mighter than the sword. It was clear to the company that this was a problem, but they would not listen to the suggestions from the staff on board. As a result, the cruise directors made some changes themselves. They planned a big party for all of the kids at the end of each cruise, and each kid was asked to bring along their comment card. After the cake, when the party was almost over, the staff would hand out pencils to all of the kids and help them mark the cards. They then checked each card carefully before they were dropped into the boxes outside of the Purser's Office. Any mistakes could be easily erased and corrected before they were submitted. This eliminated problems. Eventually the cruise ship executives came to their senses, and currently, most cruise ships only give out one card per cabin, or per family.

CHAPTER 8

Stormy Seas Ahead

It doesn't matter what time of the year, or which ocean the ship is in, foul weather can happen anytime.

Although the hurricane season in the Caribbean can be a nightmare for any ship and its crew, it's also possible to experience some of the calmest waters, provided the ship is a respectful distance from the storm.

If a hurricane is in the area, it can draw in so much energy that the rest of the surrounding seas can be calm. Like the saying, "the calm before the storm," I have seen some oceans looking like a sheet of glass, with a hurricane only one hundred miles away.

***

Having worked on a cruise ship for almost fifteen years, I ran into my fair share of bad weather—even a hurricane or two. I was in a storm off the coast of Alaska and there were two hurricanes in the Caribbean. One of those hurricanes was the worst storm I can ever remember.

It started out just like any other cruise, except the captain was concerned about a big storm heading towards Trinidad and Tobago. The winds were about fifty miles an hour, so it was still a tropical storm. Although we were sailing out of Miami, we would only go as far as St. Thomas, but the captain had a feeling—call it a sailor's intuition—that it would be a big one. All indications were that it would graze past Trinidad and head north, gaining strength out in the warm Caribbean Sea and heading up towards the Virgin Islands. So he was very concerned, indeed.

The first couple of days went well. Our first port of call was Puerto Plata, in the Dominican Republic. The weather couldn't have been better. There were calm waters, a warm, sunny, blue sky, and everything seemed perfect. No one except the captain was even thinking of the storm that was brewing some eight hundred miles south of us.

We left the port of Miami around 5:00 p.m. and headed to Puerto Rico, about three hundred miles south of us. We had very smooth sailing that night. I remember going up on deck after dinner and standing on the back of the ship looking down at the water. It was like a sheet of glass with no wind and a beautiful full moon dancing on the water. No one would have ever believed there was a raging storm heading in the ship's direction.

The next day, we arrived in San Juan, Puerto Rico. It looked like another great day, but I noticed the wind picking up. All of the passengers were up early to watch the ship enter the port, passing the great fort on our left. Many of them were catching a late breakfast up on deck. It took the captain a little longer than usual to dock the twenty-three thousand ton ship, as the wind was pushing her away from the dock. You could hear the ship growling as it struggled to ease itself closer and closer to the pier. As soon as they could, the longshoremen pulled the heavy ropes over the bollards, then the sailors on board started the motors to wind in the ropes, and they moved closer to the pier. As they attached the last rope to the pier, the ship was ready for the lowering of the gangway.

The first people to enter the ship were a couple of Immigration and Customs officers. Their job was to make sure all of the paperwork was correct, and the passenger and crew counts were correct, before they could let anyone disembark the vessel. They also checked with the ship's doctor to make sure there was no one on board with any contagious diseases. After everything checked out, then the first passenger could disembark.

As the day progressed, the captain was constantly watching the progress of the storm. With winds up to 76 miles per hour, Hurricane Dennis was heading our way. Later that day, when everyone was back on board, the captain decided, by his calculations, we would still be okay to make the quick trip overnight to St. Thomas. The storm would still be over two hundred miles away from us when we would arrive at the port of Charlotte Amalie.

Although the priority for the captain is always the safety of the passengers, crew, and his ship, he is still under an obligation to the company to complete the voyage, as he is in constant contact with them the entire time. Although the captain of any ship should have the final say, there are some companies that call the shots and make the captains do things they would not normally do.

Some companies are only thinking of the bottom line and not the safety of everyone on board. It's like throwing the dice and hoping for a good outcome.

We arrived at the entrance to Charlotte Amalie and waited for the pilot to come on board. As he and the captain talked for a moment, they both agreed to dock the ship and be ready to leave earlier than scheduled, if needed, as the whole island was on alert due to the impending storm. Many islanders were already removing their boats from the water, and those who couldn't were adjusting their lines to secure their boats as well as they could.

As we were about to dock, the passengers and crew were advised by the captain to stay close to the shore, as the captain would give one long blast of the ship's horn. This would be the sign that the ship needed to leave and everyone needed to get back on board as quickly as they could.

As it turned out, the hurricane had picked up speed the night before and was heading towards St. Thomas at a rate of 15 miles per hour. The outer bands of the storm were only 50 miles from us, so the captain decided to leave the island immediately, which meant no one would go ashore that day.

Within the hour, we were heading north, away from the storm, doing about 18 knots, about 80% of the ship's full speed. We were trying to outrun the storm that was catching up to us, which was traveling at some 20 miles per hour. We had to reach the Puerto Rican trench and cross it before the storm got too close. The trench is the second deepest water in the ocean, some fourteen thousand feet deep; it is also where the warm Caribbean seas meet the cooler Atlantic Ocean. It creates a strong current and some choppy seas on a normal day, but this was no normal cruise. It would be very difficult to maneuver the ship through the trench during a hurricane.

It was a rough night. The entire crew was asked to secure their areas, which meant that everyone was to tie down everything that could possibly move. No one got much sleep that night as we prepared for the storm. The seas swirled up and the ship rolled and swayed.

The next morning, Hurricane Dennis had reached the shores of St. Thomas and they were getting battered by the wind, as it was gushing over 100 miles per hour along with thirty-foot waves bashing the shore.

We had traveled a hundred miles during the night, away from St. Thomas, and at 8:00 a.m., the weather was deteriorating every minute. Overnight, the captain had ordered all doors leading out to the decks to be locked. The winds were reaching some 65 miles an hour, and if anyone was standing on deck, they would be blown overboard. The waves were hitting the large windows in the restaurant some sixty feet above sea level. It was very difficult to walk around without bouncing off the walls. The captain kept making announcements to all passengers, telling them to stay in their cabins. He continued to assure everyone that the ship was safe and we would get through the storm.

By this point, the eye of Hurricane Dennis was some 40 miles from us, and we were feeling the full effects of the outer bands of the storm. It was still heading our way, and all the captain could do was hold a course that would face the ship's bow into the waves as he tried to ride it out.

That night it was only getting worse. Although we could not hear the storm through the heavy metal and glass, we could feel all the effects of it. The ship was riding

up and down the 50 foot waves and rocking from side to side, groaning and grinding, like the sound of twisted metal straining against itself. The wood interior was making cracking sounds as it struggled with the forces of nature. Down below, as I lay awake in my bed, I could hear the propellers racing, as they lifted out of the water. Then there would be a shudder and a crash of thunder as the bottom of the ship slammed down on the ocean. This would happen throughout the night.

During the night, a wave hit one of the restaurant windows and shattered the three quarter inch thick glass into million of diamonds. The crew quickly boarded it up with sheets of plywood to stop the wind and water from getting inside. There was also a piano that was not tied down that went racing across the ballroom at a terrific force and smashed against the stage, breaking into a million pieces, like a box of matches.

The second day at sea, I woke up after getting some sleep to find the ship was still. There was no motion and the noises were gone. I immediately got out of bed and headed up to the dining room to see where we were. When I reached the dining room, I looked out of the window and saw a patch of blue sky and calm waters. A moment later, the captain made an announcement I wish I had not heard, saying, "Good morning, ladies and gentlemen. We made it through the worst of the storm last night; however, what you see now is the center of the storm. Yes, we are in the eye of Hurricane Dennis, and that's why there is virtually no wind and the sea is relatively calm. This will only last thirty minutes as the storm is outrunning us. We will experience the other side of the storm soon. The winds will go in the opposite direction."

No sooner had the captain finished his announcement than the weather changed again, and within less than the hour we were in the thick of it once more. The waves started rising again, and the ship listed to one side as the captain struggled to face the 70 ton vessel into the waves and winds, rising onto a wave and crashing down again. The ship would shudder and shake, and I was wondering how long the ship could put up with so much strain on it.

We went through another night of it, and by the next morning, the storm had passed and it was like nothing had happened. The water was still churning, but we were through the worst of it. There was no time to rest, however, as we all had to go and check out our departments for any repairs and cleanup that needed to be done. We continued the cruise as if nothing had happened.

It was one of the worst storms I have been in, and it was touch and go for a while, but with a good commander at the helm, we all made it through safely. No casualties were reported, but lots of damage to the ship occurred. While that can always be repaired, a life cannot. I gained a lot of respect for the captain that week.

CHAPTER 9

Romance on the High Seas

I couldn't write a book about life on a cruise ship without putting in a chapter about romance at sea. Romance between passengers and passengers, passengers and crew, crew and crew members—none of it discriminates.

When I joined the cruise ship in the early 1980s, no one had heard of AIDS, and sex was commonplace. Back then, about 90% of all crew members were male and about a third of them were gay, and with only 10% female, the rest of the playing field were the passengers. Many single girls were traveling on cruises because their friends were telling them about all of the European men working on the ships, and to the European men, American girls were easier than their European counterparts. For many young American girls, it was okay to fool around because they were away from home and nobody would ever know what happened on a cruise. It was a bit like the ads for Las Vegas—what happens on the cruise ship stays on the cruise ship.

On my first cruise, when I was a busboy, I was approached by a woman at my table. She was traveling with her mother and was at least 10 years older than I was, but she asked me straight out to meet her in her cabin. I asked my waiter what he thought and he said to be very careful since I didn't know my way around the ship yet, and if I got caught, I would be fired. I needed my job more than the girl, so I turned down the offer carefully. But there would be many more offers that I took later, when I was more familiar with the layout of the ship and the rules.

On one occasion, I had a roommate who found twins and he needed some help. I was sitting in my underwear watching television in my cabin when the door busted open and a young girl around 22 was pushed into the room. The door slammed shut behind her. She stood there and I apologized to her and immediately put on a shirt and a pair of shorts.

I offered her a seat and tried some small talk, but I wasn't very good at it. I was thinking she was there waiting for my roommate, but what I didn't know at the time was that he was trying to separate them so he could be with one, so he sent the other one to me. I realized it when about an hour passed and the cabin door opened and Manuel, my room mate, was standing in the doorway he look at both of us and said "what the hell are you both doing" so he turned away and closed the door then we both got down to business. I ended up with her all cruise and he with her twin sister. To this day we often wonder if they ever switched on us, but we'll never know.

Years later I was on a ship with Manual, we had two separate cabins but with a joining bathroom in between and on one night I was in my cabin watching a movie when I heard a knock on the bathroom door, when I opened it there was a young lady struggling to put on her cloths and asked me the way out, I showed her the front door that leaded out to the hallway, she left quietly. The next morning I asked Manuel, what had happened, he told me he had two sittings that night one girl at 11pm and a second one at 1am, but the second girl showed up to his door early and the only thing he could do was get the first girl to leave his cabin though the bathroom into my cabin, as this was happening the second girl was entering his cabin from the hallway. We had many a great experience together. We became very good friends and in-fact he was the best man at my wedding.

The cruise line frowned on crew hooking up with passengers mainly because of the possibilities of lawsuits. There was the fact was there was one girl for every fifty boys who worked on the ship so no matter what rules were made, the crew would always beat the system and take a chance trying not to be caught, as it was an offense that would get a crew member fired, if one was caught with a passenger.

On one ship, I remember the captain offered the security personnel one hundred dollars if they caught a waiter in a guest cabin. One story a waiter told me was about another waiter, Peter, visiting a passenger in her cabin, and after a glass or two of wine and doing their business, he asked the girl to look outside of her cabin to make sure no security was waiting outside; she opened the door and looked to the left down a long corridor and saw nothing. Then she looked to the right. At the end of the corridor, she could see a gentleman in a white uniform holding a walkie talkie to his mouth. She quickly closed the door and sat on the end of the bed. She said it wasn't safe, so they had another drink or two. By that time, it was 2:00 a.m. and Peter wanted to get some sleep before starting work the next day. She waited about half an hour and tried again to open the door slowly. She looked to the right, and the same officer was standing at the end of the corridor. He must have heard them as he passed the cabin earlier and was waiting to catch the waiter and claim his reward of one hundred dollars She quickly jumped back into the room, and Peter tried to figure out what to do

"I will have to make a run for it," Peter said.

"Wait," said the girl, as she grabbed the blanket off of the bed. She then threw it over Peter's head, opened the door, and Peter ran out into the corridor, immediately turning left, and ran down the hall and out of sight before the officer had a chance to see who it was under the blanket. Suffice it to say, he didn't make his hundred dollars that night.

I have known of many couples who were on the cruise for their honeymoon and after a day or two, one of the waiters would end up sleeping with the wife. On one occasion, it was mid-summer and there was a beautiful couple on board. They had just gotten married in Miami and were on the cruise for their honeymoon. That first night at dinner they celebrated with a small cake and all of the waiters gathered around them to sing Happy Honeymoon. As they were leaving the dining room arm in arm, I saw a very good looking Italian waiter slip a piece of paper into the bride's hand. She quickly closed her hand as they walked out into the hall outside of the dining room.

Later on that night, I saw the groom at the midnight buffet on his own. I asked him,

"Where is your beautiful bride?"

He replied, "I'm not sure. I left her in the nightclub. She wanted to dance more, and I was hungry, so I came down to eat."

The next day there was a commotion and we heard he was up all night looking for his wife. Around 3:00 a.m. he called the bridge and told the officer on duty that his wife was missing. They searched everywhere and could not find her. Later the next morning she turned up at their cabin still in her wedding dress from the night before. Her husband was so mad that he didn't know what happened to her.

She had spent the night in the waiter's cabin, the one who handed her the note. I guess the husband never found out because, according to the waiter, she spent several nights with him and told him when she got back to the U.S., she would get a divorce from her husband.

There was a waiter called Roberto from Italy. He was not the typical Italian; rather, he was short, chubby, and not too good-looking, but he made up for it with his personality. He would always end up with two or three girls a week, every week. I remember asking him one day how he did it. He told me that if one asked enough girls, he would be bound to get lucky. He would stand at the dining room door each night after dinner and ask every girl leaving if they would like to have a drink with him. He would collect several room numbers a night.

Another waiter told me a story about how he ended up sleeping with a mother and daughter—not at the same time, but on the same cruise. It started one day on a cruise where there was a young mother and her sixteen-year-old daughter at his table. On the second day of the cruise, he met the mother for a drink and they both ended up in his cabin. A couple of days later, after several visits to his cabin, the mother asked him to have sex with her daughter. He was stunned to have such a thing proposed; however, she explained how she knew her daughter would have sex with someone on the cruise, and she would feel better knowing who it was. So, a day later, her daughter showed up at his cabin door for a visit. He told me later that all three of them spent the last night of the cruise together—with the mother watching her daughter having sex with him.

One cruise we had these two big girls, and I mean big—they both must have weighed at least 300 pounds each, but they had beautiful faces. They were about 30 years old and were friendly, getting to know everyone on the cruise. Their goal was to have sex with as many crew members as they could. They had been on the same ship many times before and spent up to 20 cruises on that ship, as they always had a good time on board.

My friend from Ireland, Patrick, was servicing one of these girls, and the interesting thing was that he was about five foot nine and weighed about one hundred and forty pounds. Patrick had no shame.

A good friend of mine, James, from England, met up with one purser, Jessica; she was also from England, and they were inseparable. They met one night in the disco. James said it was love at first sight. When they were not working, they were always together, whether it was at the beach or in the disco. Her roommate moved out of the cabin so they both could share the cabin.

After a year on board, they both signed off together, and they decided to meet each other's parents when they got back to England.

After six glorious weeks together, they were planning to get married, but they both decided to go back to the ship for another contract each to save some more money so they could put down a good deposit on a house. They had it all planned.

When they returned to Miami, however, the company separated them. Jessica would have to go onto the ship that did a two-week cruise and James the one-week ship. That meant they would only meet in Miami every two weeks. They were not happy with this and pleaded with the personnel manager to put them on the same ship.

"No," he replied, "it is all set. I can't change it now. You will both have to live with it."

As the weeks passed and they got to spend about two hours with each other every two weeks, James bought a ring in the Bahamas and the next time the ships met, he planned to propose to Jessica.

It was a glorious morning when we arrived back in Miami. We were finishing up breakfast in the dining room and I looked over at James. He had the biggest smile on his face, and he could not wait to get off of the ship to see Jessica.

One hour later, he was running off the crew gangway and down the pier to our sister ship that was docked some eight hundred yards behind us. He sprinted the entire way, dashing up the other gangway, and without stopping, he handed the officer his crew pass. Next he ran down a few flights of stairs and along a corridor until he was standing outside of Jessica's cabin. He had not taken a breath since he left our ship, so he took a moment to compose himself before knocking at the door. He checked to make sure he still had the small box in his left pocket; it was still there. He then opened the door and entered the cabin. He walked over to her bed and pulled the curtain back and to his surprise, she was not alone. Jessica jumped up, covered herself, and said, "What are you doing here so early?"

James replied, "What the hell are you doing? Who is that?"

"I'm her boyfriend," the voice came from under the sheets.

"No, you're not. I'm her boyfriend," James replied.

Jessica said, "James, you need to leave now."

"Don't worry, I am leaving, leaving for good," he said, and then turned and walked out of the room, dejected.

As he walked off the gangway, his mind was a mess. It turned his world upside down. He thought about how and when this could have happened as he walked along the pier. He put his hand into his left pocket took out the small box and tossed it at the ship. It hit the side of the ship and disappeared into the grey sea below.

James and Jessica never saw each other again. James stayed on ships for a few more years and dated no one. Although, I believe he is now a happily married with two children back in England. I don't know what happened to Jessica. We never kept in touch after that day in Miami.

A year later, I was promoted to Assistant Dining Room Manager. We had a group of students on for spring break, and this was the first time I found out what spring break was all about in the States. The first morning we were at sea, sailing to Puerto Plata in the Dominican Republic. It was a beautiful day, about eighty degrees with blue skies and a gentle breeze on deck. I was on duty at the pool when I saw a couple of officers running towards the sun deck. Curious to see what was going on; I followed the officers up to the sun deck, and when we got there, we found several of the young girls from the spring break group dancing on the deck chairs, waving their bikini tops in the air. It wouldn't have been so bad if there were no other passengers there' with their small children, but there were, and the mothers were covering the kids' eyes while the fathers were taking photos. The officers were chasing the girls around the deck, pleading with them to put their tops back on.

Later that night when they came into the dining room, they were singing and dancing with the waiters. Some girls were asking the waiters to meet them later on in their cabins. I walked over to one table to get the girls to sit down; they had been drinking all day long up at the lido bar. I heard two voices say, "Hey, handsome. What's your name, you with the bars on your shoulder?"

I turned around to see two beautiful girls sitting at the table. They both had long blonde hair, blue eyes, and big smiles. They were wearing white T-shirts and short blue skirts. They could not have been more than 20 years old. I was 26 at the time. They looked at me and together said, "Want to party later?" They both opened their legs to show me they were not wearing any underwear.

There were several chaperones and security on board from the schools that were supposed to be in charge, but everyone was out of hand and there was no control. The officers on board had their hands full literally all cruise.

On the last night of the cruise, one officer I was talking to said, "Come, I want to show you something."

I followed him up to the promenade deck where most of the spring breakers were staying; we walked along the corridor and he stopped at one cabin. There was a handwritten sign stuck on the door. It read: "Five dollars for a blow job. Twenty-five for a shag." That was one of the wildest cruises I ever worked.

Later we found out that they had damaged many of the cabins and set off the fire extinguishers in the hallways, not to mention all of the complaints we got from the other passengers. I had heard that they paid a hefty security deposit, which, of course, they lost. The rooms that were destroyed took five weeks to repair before they could be used again.

At the beginning of one cruise, we were all sitting in the dining room waiting for the dining room manager to assign the stations when he announced that there was a woman on board sailing with six young girls all under sixteen, but they looked like they were twenty. He pointed over to their table and said that no waiter or busboy was to go near them—not even look at them, or that person would be fired. The girls would be on the second seating. That night when they came into the dining room, the girls tried to talk to every waiter who passed the table, but no one would talk to them. They were assigned the oldest waiter and busboy and didn't care to talk to them. After about three days, the lady asked to speak to the dining room manager. When he went over to talk to her, she asked how come the waiters won't talk to the girls, and how they were ignoring them. She told of being on another cruise and how every waiter came over to their table and talked to the girls and took pictures. The dining room manager replied, "I know what you are up to," and "You won't be able to do it on my ship."

She said, "Well, I never. This is the worst cruise I have ever been on and you, sir, are very rude. I will report you to the head office for this."

After the cruise was over, I was talking to the dining room manager and asked him why this table and what was the big secret.

He handed me a sheet of paper with the ship's logo on the top, in gold. This could only mean one thing: it came from the office and only from the president. It read:

"To the Captain and all Officers. From the President.

There is a lady sailing this cruise with six young girls all under sixteen. The lady's name is Mrs. ... she has sailed on other ships and cruise lines in the last year and has brought several lawsuits against the companies. They have notified us she is a professional. She encourages the girls to meet with the crew, and before anything happens, they all claim they were forced to have sex with the crew and were raped and they are all underage."

They were never seen sailing on our ships again.

CHAPTER 10

Going to Church

Long before there were casinos on cruise ships, the crew always gambled. Even when they couldn't gamble on the ship, they were visiting the casinos shoreside in Aruba, San Juan, Puerto Rico, Freeport, or Paradise Island, Bahamas. Whenever the crew had some time off, they could be found at a casino on one of these islands. The Indonesian, Chinese, and Filipino crew members, especially, had a great passion for gambling. The bad thing was that it is like any other addiction. I have seen many lives destroyed because of it.

Those who would go to the casinos would call it "going to church." I worked for a while on a ship that would be in Nassau, Bahamas every Sunday, and when any gambler was asked where they were going, they would say, "I am off to church. I hope the collection is good today." Even the taxi drivers in Nassau would know when they asked where someone wanted to go, and they would say, "Take us to church," so they would know to drop them off at the nearest casino on Paradise Island.

I worked years ago with an Italian dining room manager who spent all of his free time in a casino. I remember he would bring us along with him. There would be a stretch limo waiting for us at the bottom of the gangway. About seven of us would climb in and be whisked away to a casino on Condado Beach in San Juan. We were treated like celebrities. We would be taken to a private room in the hotel and offered a glass of champagne or a drink of our choice. Then, we would be offered a grand, sumptuous dinner that would include beluga caviar, lobster, big steaks and chocolate soufflé, or cherries jubilee with table side service, Hennessy VSOP, a rare brandy, and espresso, followed by the best hand rolled Cuban cigars. We were treated to nothing but the best, and only because the dining room manager would drop around $10,000 a night. His addiction was really bad. I watched him lose $30,000 in one night in San Juan.

This was his worst evening ever. I once asked him if I could take some of his money and put it away for him, and he agreed. So, for six months I saved about $1,000 each month for him. I would give him a receipt every time and show him the balance. After six months, he asked me for the money because he was going home, so I went to the bank and got a cashier's check for $6,000 and gave it to him.

He did not go home, though; he took a flight to the Bahamas on Chalky, an airline seaplane out of Miami, and blew the six grand in one hour. I remember when his mom got sick in Italy and he did not have a penny to get home, we all pitched in and raised the money to buy him a plane ticket to get him home to see his mom. She passed away a few days later.

Casinos were not my thing. I watched too many people work so hard on the ship only to hand it all over to the casino. Don't get me wrong; I had a few flutters on the blackjack table and at the roulette wheel, but I never lost more than a couple hundred bucks.

The Viking Crown Lounge on the Song of Norway

The Song of Norway docked in St. Thomas

The Ship's bell on the bow of the ship

Smoked Salmon cream cheese and bagels for my busboy's breakfast every morning

Carrying my first tray of sixteen dishes

Trying on the captain's jacket in the laundry

Standing on top of a glacier in Alaska

Another hard day at work

Taking the tender back from our private island

Teamwork makes the dream work

Victor, myself, and Luigi, great team

Who will be the next 007

Goofing around on the American Adventure with my dining room team
Myself, Aras, Delip, Roberto, Paulo, and Michael

And another, although there is a real $80,000 in that bag.

Hotel Manager with another
great team
on the Dolphin IV

Head waiter of the year award, with my good
friend Roberto in the background, may he rest
in peace.

Receiving my five year ring from the captain on the Sun Viking

All part of the Job, Michelle, Myself and Stacey on the Dolphin IV

The Irish Mafia with one of the Famous Irish Duo, The Clancy brothers.

A cruise reunion with my great friends Manuel, myself, Luz, Tony, and our late friend, Denzil. May he rest in peace.

The name is Bond ....James Bond.....

The Sun sets on a great career.

CHAPTER 11

The Money Makers

One of the major benefits of working on a cruise ship, apart from the travel and experience, is the money that can be made and saved because crew members don't have the usual expenses that they have on land, including rent, gas, utilities, etc.

If smart, one can stash away quite a bit of money towards a house and the future. However, some jobs are better than others for that.

I worked in the restaurant where most of the income came from guests' tips, and on a good week as a waiter, I could make a tax free $800 a week. Back in 1980, that was very good, even with working an average day of 16 hours, seven days a week. As I moved up to be head waiter, in a good week, I made $1,200, and by the time I made it to being dining room manager, I was making $2,500 per week. I knew dining room managers on larger ships who made over $3,000 per week. It seemed that the more money one made, the greedier some of those people became.

There were many managers who found additional creative ways to add to their income. One such way I found out when I was asked to take over as the dining room manager who was going on vacation for six weeks.

It was five in the afternoon. The ship was getting ready to sail on a new cruise with all new passengers, and I was up in my cabin working on the new stations for all of the waiters with the ratings from the previous cruise. There was a knock on my cabin door. When I opened it, there were three waiters standing in the hallway and they presented me with three sealed envelopes. I asked what it was all about, and they replied how they always gave the dining room manager an envelope each every week for their stations, to which I replied how that was not the way I was going to do things. I planned that everyone would be rewarded their stations based on the previous ratings like the company expected. I suggested that they return to the dining room and wait until I came down to hand out the stations. On that cruise, those three gentlemen had the lowest ratings of all eighty waiters, and so they received the smallest stations. Thus, they made the smallest tips. That is the way the system was, and it was the fairest for everyone else. Needless to say, they were not happy, and they remained that way until the dining room manager returned from his six weeks' vacation.

I will never know how much was in each envelope, but over the years I heard some waiters were paying some managers as much as $200 each week to keep a good station.

Another way that the managers used to make extra money was when a waiter wanted a day off (this only meant a lunch off in port; if a cruise ship had three stops in a week the waiters were divided up into three groups, and one group would have lunch off to go ashore, while the other two-thirds would work the buffet lunch on board). If anyone wanted an extra lunch off, they could pay another waiter to work for them. The going rate was $50; however, some ports were more expensive. A lunch off in St. Thomas could run as much as $75, while a lunch off in Barbados was $100, all for about three hours work. I used to work for a few waiters so I could put away some extra money. I knew some waiters who would pay out almost as much as half of their weekly tips to others who worked for them.

When the managers found out about this, they decided to get in on the act. They would ask the same waiters if they wanted to be off to pay the dining room manager the money directly, and he would cover their shift. Then the manager would find a waiter who came late to work, and as a punishment, he would make him work the extra shift and the manager would pocket the cash. I knew managers who made an extra $800 to $1,200 per month doing just that.

One dining room manager I knew was bringing in waiters from his hometown, getting them jobs with the company, and in turn, they would pay him as much as $5,000 for the job.

Back in the earlier years, all dining room managers had to work the restaurant. This meant they would have a station of their own to cover and try to oversee all other areas. After several years, all of the dining room managers decided they would split their sections with the head waiters and this would free them up to oversee the whole dining room. For this, they would collect as much as $300 from each head waiter per cruise, regardless of how much the head waiter made. On some of the larger ships where they could have as many as six to eight head waiters, paying $300 each week, well, it added up quite quickly.

The big money makers were the cruise directors. From horse racing to tours and bingo, there were plenty of ways for them to make lots of extra money during a cruise. They were the masters at this back in the early 1980s. I knew some cruise directors with three or four homes around the world, and they made as much as $8000 to $10,000 per week, which was a substantial amount at the time. They were like royalty, movie stars at the top of their game.

They were paid a salary from the company of about $5000 per month. The rest came from all of the activities on board and from the shops they would mention in their talks. During each cruise, the cruise director or assistant would have a talk about the ports of call. Usually this would happen the first day at sea before the ship would make its first port of call. He would tell about all of the benefits of taking a tour that the ship would offer, and deter passengers from making their own arrangements with the tour operators on land. He would also recommend several shops to shop at, while warning to stay away from others. The passengers were all taking notes, writing all he was saying, as the cruise director's word was his bond. No one doubted him or his advice.

Immediately after this important talk, the ship's tour desk was open and everyone was told that all of the best tours would sell out quickly. There were two very important goals for this talk—one was to sell out all tours on board the ship. This was so passengers wouldn't buy any when they got to the islands on shore, and thus the company would make money as the markup was huge. The cruise director would get a cut of all of the tours sold on board. He would also get a share from the tour operators for sending the passengers to them. Another way the cruise director would make extra money was from the shops on each island. The cruise director would collect an envelope from each store owner based on the amount each store sold the previous cruise. This envelope was a tip for the cruise director to keep, and for anyone who has ever been on a cruise to St. Thomas and Puerto Rico and seen all of the shops, it's easy to imagine how much money the cruise director could potentially collect from every store.

Years later, when the shoreside office found out about what the cruise director was doing, they fired all of the directors and made their own arrangements to collect the money for the company. They hired all new staff, too. During each cruise, there would be several activities that the cruise director would arrange for the passengers in order to give them something to do during long days at sea, from horse racing and bingo, to betting on whether the ship would arrive in port on time, although the latter was usually only on the long transatlantic crossings and world tours more than the shortened cruises in the Caribbean.

Horse racing was a betting game. There were six wooden horses and a roll out mat with six rows and twenty spaces on each row. Each horse had a name like Irisheyes, the Italian stallion, etc. and before each race, the cruise director would open up the betting. Each interested passenger would place a bet on their favorite horse, and after all of the money was collected, the cruise director would announce the odds and would know instantly, exactly by the betting, which horse he needed to call the winner for him to make the most money. Half of the money would go to the company; the other half would go to the cruise staff.

The cruise director would start the race and he would have a dice cage which he would shake up and call out what horse and how many spaces the horse would move. He occasionally showed the dice to an audience member, but right from the start he knew the horse that needed to win, the horse with the least pay out; it was all good fun and the passengers were having a great time. The cruise director would end up adding another one thousand dollars to his bank account.

Bingo would start with a small game at the beginning of the cruise and build up to a final big bingo game at the end of the cruise. There would be a small payout the first day and the money would all accumulate up to the final game. Again, the payout would be small compared to the money collected, and again, half would go to the house and the other half would go to the cruise director. There was no paperwork or real way for the company to know exactly how much money was actually collected each week. Although, when the money was collected from both the horse racing and bingo games, a member of the purser's department was present, but they were likely in on the take as well.

Almost everyone was in on some scheme. I remember when I first started as a waiter, in order to get the bread hot out of the oven first, waiters paid a dollar to someone in the kitchen to get it that way. If waiters didn't want to wait for boiled eggs, they paid a dishwasher a dollar so he would do it. To get dishes cleaned quickly in order to set the tables quickly before the next seating, the kitchen porter could be paid a few dollars to ensure the person paying got their stuff first. Those who didn't pay would have to wait till the end, and then sometimes they would find silverware missing or a few plates gone.

The same thing happened in the laundry. The laundry area on most ships is run by the Chinese. They even had their own kitchen in the laundry section of the ship where they made their own food each day. If someone got to know them well, like I did, they would send an invitation to eat with them. This made it clear to anyone invited that they were in their good graces; however, the normal turnaround time for the clothes and sheets was four days. This was not bad, but if a crew member wanted it sooner, say in two days, that person would pay the head laundry guy an extra five dollars per week. The fact was that it only took two days to do all of the laundry, so the crew that wouldn't pay the extra five dollars had their clothes hidden away for the additional two days.

There were also people who could be paid to clean cabins and change sheets every week. If there were four people in a cabin, these people would collect three dollars each and someone would do the work. It was a good deal because each week the captain would inspect every crew cabin, and if it wasn't clean, the cabin would be fined and each person would get a warning. Therefore, it was better to pay someone to do this, and the person cleaning the cabin was a cook or cleaner who only made about $500 a month and was cleaning about 10 to 15 rooms per week, so he could easily make another $120 to $150 per week. This would essentially and potentially double his income each month.

If someone was a waiter and wanted to have every port off, there were people who could be paid to work instead. Some ports cost more than others. In order to be off for lunch for two hours, or to go ashore, or even just get an extra few hours' sleep, someone could be paid $40 for time off in the Dominican Republic. However, if one wanted to be off in Barbados or St. Thomas or even St. Maarten, it could cost up to $100, which was not bad for two hours' work.

I personally made extra money that way. There were a couple of waiters I could rely on each and every week for an extra $140. I called them my regulars. I remember one morning we were in St. Thomas and I was working for my regular waiter for lunch. It was a nice, easy one hundred dollars. I went down to my cabin around ten o'clock after breakfast for a short rest before lunch at 11:30. I was just about to put my head down on my pillow when there was a knock on the door. Another waiter was standing outside, and he desperately needed someone to work for him at lunch. At first I said no, and then I asked him where his station was, quickly calculating that maybe I could work both stations, collect two hundred dollars, and no one would find out. I then accepted his offer and went up to the dining room to get both stations ready. I calculated that my first station would fill up first and then about an hour later when all of the tours got back to the ship, the second would fill up.

I only had to pull it off before the dining room manager found out. During the service, one other waiter saw what was going on and when he approached me, I was worried he was going to give me up, but all he did was smile and tell me that if I needed help, to let me know, as if to say he wanted me to succeed. Several times during service, the head waiter would look over at me suspiciously, but he didn't say anything. Needless to say, I pulled it off. As far as I know, I was the first to work two stations in one lunch and maybe to this day I still hold that record. That night, I collected my two hundred dollars. Years later, when I look at my house in Ireland or my apartment in Miami, I thank those other waiters repeatedly.

***

Over the years, I saw many ways for people to make extra money on the ships. Some just got too greedy, and eventually were caught. One such case was an operations manager who had worked on the ships for many years as a dining manager and invented all of the ways to make an extra buck or two. Working ashore in the head office, he saw another way to make extra money.

In nearly every country, there were agents for the ships. Their job was to look for new waiters to work on the ships. They would often ask each waiter for a couple of hundred dollars—a processing fee, they would call it—but it went straight into their pockets. He decided to eliminate the middleman and hire waiters himself. He would hire waiters from his home country, and told them if they gave him one thousand dollars, he would promise them a job. He would hire about ten waiters per month. That's an extra ten thousand per month in his pocket, tax free. Everything was going well with his plan, and he may have never gotten caught, except for one time that ruined it for him. After a week on board, one of the waiters he hired was fired by one of the dining room managers on the ship. The waiter went to the office to complain to someone, but the someone he spoke to was one of the CEOs. After explaining that he just paid someone in the company one thousand dollars for the job and was fired after a week, the CEO asked the waiter who that person was, and the next day the operations manager was fired himself.

I made good money as a waiter in my early years on the ships; I earned it the honest way, through hard work and long hours. Back in the early 1980s, I was working as a waiter and I had the largest station allowed. As a result of my high ratings, I had 20 guests at each seating for a total of 40 people, and each couple was given the recommendation to tip $28 for the entire week, but many of them tipped $40 or $50 for the week.

I was a good saver and didn't have many expenses on the ship; I had a room and board, so I didn't need to have a home or rent to worry about, and I didn't have to buy any food or have a car, so all of the major expenses I would normally have had on land, I didn't have. I would buy some soap, shampoo, and toothpaste, as well as a couple of beers in the crew bar, but that was about it. So, after two years, I had accumulated enough money to buy a house for my mom back in Ireland.

CHAPTER 12

A New Home

One day while I was on the phone with my dad, he told me that the landlord was going to raise their rent by as much as ten times what it was at that time. My dad was so worried and didn't want to tell my mom. He was about to retire and didn't know what to do. I told him not to worry, that I had saved some money during the past two years on the ship and that I wanted to buy a home in Ireland, anyway. I told him I would take some time off from the ship in a couple of weeks, and he and I would look around for a house that both of them could live in for as long as they were alive, rent free. I told him to keep it a secret from Mom, so we could surprise her.

I took a break from the ship for six weeks, and as soon as I got home to Ireland, I started looking for a home in a price range I could afford. I narrowed it down to a few. There was one older house that was nice, but it was not near shops or transportation, and would have needed some repairs, and as my mom and dad were nearing retirement,

I didn't want them to be too isolated from either. The second was tiny and not yet completed. The third was a new home in a small town called Greystones in Co Wicklow. Just south of Dublin. It was a show house, and the first home I had ever seen with a bathroom off of the master bedroom. It had a great kitchen with all of the appliances included, and a big back garden which my mom would enjoy because the two things she liked to do most were gardening and cooking.

The kitchen was fitted with everything she would need, and the garden was big enough to grow some fruit and vegetables and still have room for a flower garden. It was in a suitable area near the village and close to the train station.

I told my dad, "I think I've found the one." So I instructed him to get Mom ready for a drive in the country.

It was a sunny Sunday afternoon, and I decided to take them both to all three homes just to get a feel for which one they would like, My mom thought I was just looking; she had no idea that I would buy one of them in a few weeks before I returned to the ship.

After seeing all three, I asked my mom which one she liked, and of course Mom being Mom, said, "I would be happy with any of them, if only I could win the lottery."

First thing Monday morning, I contacted the builders to find out how I could buy the last one we had seen; he put me in touch with a solicitor who would help me put the paperwork together and make the deal; I met with him in Dublin later on that week and started the paperwork. After that, I didn't hear from him for two weeks, and, by that point, I had only two weeks left before I would have to go back to work on the ship, so I went to the solicitor's office to ask him what I needed to do next. I told him I would leave Ireland in a week (not the two weeks I had left) and that if everything was not ready in a week, the deal was off. He said he understood and the only thing that he wanted to know from me was which bank was loaning me the money, as that was the only thing holding everything up.

"Loan?" I said. "What loan? Hell, I am going to write you a check for the full amount now." He almost fell out of his chair.

He said to me, "You must make good money on the ships, because I have been a solicitor for ten years and I have never seen money like that."

I wrote him the check, and before the week was out, he called me into his office to sign a couple more papers and handed me the keys to my first home. I called my dad right away. He was still at work, and I told him, "Well, Dad, you don't have to worry anymore. I have the keys to a brand new home."

When we both got home that night, I told my mom I wanted her to see one more house, so after dinner she took off her apron, brushed her hair, got into the car, and we were off.

As I drove up to the house, my mom said, "Didn't we see this one already, and anyway, there won't be anyone at this time of night to show it to us." As we walked up to the house, I took the keys out of my pocket, and as my mom looked over at me, I opened the front door. I told her, "They sent me the key earlier." We entered the house and made our way to the kitchen, and I again asked my mom what she thought of the house. She said, "I would give anything to have a kitchen like this," at which time I handed her the keys and said, "Well, it's yours now."

She went into shock and then the tears started flowing. It was hard for me not to follow, and I soon started crying, too. Then, as only mothers can do, she gave me one of her big hugs, although I could tell this one was bigger and longer than normal. She whispered in my ear, "How can we ever repay you?" to which I replied, "You already have."

***

When we returned to the old house later that night, there was a message waiting for me. The cruise line wanted me to return to work the very next day.

The next morning, as I was about to leave for the airport, I took one last look around the old house, with all its dampness and mold on the walls, thinking, *Thank God my parents don't have to live here anymore.*

Over the next few months, my mom and dad moved into their new home. However, it would be fourteen months before I would spend my first night in Greystones.

CHAPTER 13

Linga Linga

The most fun way to make extra money as the restaurant manager was with the "Linga Linga," which means the beer cart. One of the side jobs for a waiter, and some say the best, was to supply beer and soda to all of the dining room staff. He would buy cases of beer and soda from the provision master (store keeper) at the beginning of each cruise for about 30 cents for a can of beer and 20 cents for sodas. It was all duty free back then, and he would store it in a cart with ice and serve it to the waiters after breakfast, lunch, and dinner each day for a dollar each. He would keep track of what each waiter drank, and at the end of each cruise would collect the money. Many times, the waiters who drank several beers a day would have a few extra drinks added to the list when it came time to collect the money. He knew they would not be keeping an account of exactly how many they were regularly having.

Several times a month, if we pulled in good ratings, the food and beverage manager would send down ten cases of beer to the dining room for a job well done. However, this was also added to the Linga Linga and to the profits of the dining room manager. The waiter who had this side job made a little extra money himself and usually drank for free, and the dining room manager pocketed the profits as much as $300 to $1000 a week. It was only years later that I realized why so many dining room managers like to have Irish waiters on their team. Not only were they good at making the ratings, but they were equally good at drinking beer.

I remember on one ship how the dining room manager would offer a case of beer to the waiter who sold the least amount of lobster that cruise, as this would save the company money as well. It became a great competition for each cruise. Some waiters would go as far as telling their passengers that the lobster was bad, it had an unpleasant smell, and not to order it.

I was a head waiter at the time and noticed that it was the same group winning the case of beer each cruise. This group was comprised of three English waiters and four Irish waiters, so I watched them carefully the next cruise.

On the night that lobster was on the menu, three of the waiters were in my section, so I watched them take the orders, head to the kitchen, and serve the food. At the end of the night, and after all of the orders were counted, the dining room manager announced one of the waiters who was in my section as the winner of the case of beer. That night I walked over to the group of waiters. I had worked as a waiter with some of them in the past, and as I approached them, they were whispering to each other. They knew I was on to them before I even told them so. I said, "I do not know how you are doing it, but I will find out."

As Patrick handed me a beer, he said, "I don't know what you're talking about," and they all laughed as I walked away.

The next cruise came, and with it Lobster Night. I was ready this time; I had five of the group in my section that week, and as I watched them take the orders, I was passing by Patrick's tables and overheard a guest ordering lobster. Later, I headed off to the kitchen to watch Patrick pick up his order, and I noticed he didn't pick up any lobster. I followed him back to his station, and at a distance watched him serve his guests; he got to the last person, the one I overheard order lobster, and just then one of the other waiters came over and switched his plate for Patrick's, and then Patrick served the lobster to his last guest. I rounded the corner and said, "Ah, ah, I now know how you're doing it."

Patrick turned to me and said, "I don't know what you mean."

"I'll tell you later," I replied.

That night after dinner, Patrick won the case of beer. Afterward, I walked over to their table and sat down. I said, "You all take your orders and then meet up in the kitchen, and at the same time you check with each other to see who has the least lobster ordered, then you swap out the lobster with a steak or chicken with the other person so every cruise one of you has no lobster on their list, then when you get back into the dining room you switch the order back so everyone gets what they need. The chef and the dining room manager count all the tickets up at the end of the night and one of you always wins."

They looked stunned that anyone could have found out their system.

Patrick turned to me and said, "Well done, you've got us, and if you keep our secret and don't tell anyone, we will include you in our free beer." I agreed, but I was just happy to have figured it out for myself. I enjoyed the beer and keeping their secret. I don't believe anyone ever found out or suspected anything after that.

***

One day I was on a ship that stopped at a private island off the coast of Punta Cana in the Dominican Republic. It was our first visit and there was not much set up on the island except for a beach, so our passengers had to return to the ship for lunch. The tender ride was only five minutes, so they were able to go back and forth easily. The tender is a small boat that takes the guests from the big ship to the harbor back in the day they often used one of the lifeboats.

I was sitting in my office on the ship when I heard a knock on the door. When I opened it, there standing in the doorway was the waiter who was in charge of the Linga Linga. He was out of breath as he explained to me how the crew and passengers were thirsty from the heat and could he have my permission to take a large cooler over to the island.

I said sure, so long as we didn't get into any trouble. He and another waiter loaded up a cooler full of beer, water, and soft drinks before proceeding down the gangway to meet the tender. When he got to the island to serve the crew, all of the passengers started to gather around and they too wanted to buy some refreshments, so he started to serve them, too. After half an hour, he was running out of everything, so he quickly returned and filled up the cooler again and headed back to the island a second time. The passengers and crew were very happy; however, the owners of the island were not, so they forbid us from doing it the next cruise. It wasn't long after this that they set up their own bar on the island. It was good while it lasted. We made some nice money that cruise.

CHAPTER 14

Drug Runners

During the 1970s and 1980s, drugs started to be more prevalent, and the drug lords were trying all kinds of ways to get their products into the United States, including the use of cruise ships.

With some 20 cruise ships traveling from the Caribbean back to U.S. ports each week, it was not surprising that they would find this a great way to traffic drugs to the U.S.

One way they used was to offer a couple of young girls a free cruise. In exchange for the free cruise, the girls would pick up a shipment of marijuana from Jamaica and hand it over to someone waiting at the Port of Miami when the cruise was over. It sounds simple, and sometimes it was that easy.

However, it was not long before the U.S. Drug Enforcement Agency set up a deal with Jamaica and they had agents in Jamaica at the ports of Ocho Rios and Montego Bay to stop the drugs from leaving the island.

I remember one time we were leaving Miami on a week cruise, with plans to stop at Grand Cayman, Cozumel, and Ocho Rios, Jamaica, returning to Miami the following Saturday. There were two young girls in their late teens or early twenties, college age, and, of course, all of the waiters were going over to their table to talk to them, but there was something different about them. They kept to themselves and didn't even mix with the other passengers. They showed up to the dining room the first night and then we didn't see them again until we reached Jamaica.

It was about 4:00 p.m. in the afternoon and the ship was getting ready to leave Jamaica. I was coming back from the beach, and as I approached the gangway, I saw the two girls. This time, though, they were both in handcuffs and crying. There were two large men wearing black shirts with the Letters U.S.D.E.A. (United States Drug Enforcement Agency) on their backs, who were standing beside them. It appeared they were asking them questions and writing down their answers. They arrested them in Jamaica and the girls didn't get to finish the cruise.

This happened so many times in the early 1980s that we would have bets in the dining room when we would see a couple of young girls on their own and keeping to themselves. We tried to guess who would be arrested in Jamaica and who wouldn't.

Several crew members also took part in the same smuggling activity, some successfully and some not. I learned of one waiter in the 1970s who worked on the ship or a couple of years only to retire back in his home country of Spain. He bought a large farm, a brand new Mercedes, and a home for his family. I was told he made over 150 runs from Port Antonio, Jamaica to Miami, Florida and was never caught. I'm not sure how he could just stop. I guess he could leave the U.S. without being caught by either federal agents or drug gangs.

I have also heard of many who were not so lucky, mostly caught by the D.E.A. in Miami. Some were caught by the drug gangs when they were trying to stop, but they knew too much and the gangs were afraid they might turn against them and tell the D.E.A. all they knew, giving up valuable names and information. Then, there would only be two choices—to continue trafficking, or to end up dead somewhere at the bottom of the ocean. Some traffickers would send a decoy. There would be a newbie who would get caught in Miami with a small amount of drugs on him. Then, while everyone was watching him, a bigger load would slip through without anyone noticing. It got so bad that in the early 1980s, the D.E.A. would surprise the ships when they arrived back in Miami by boarding the ship with sniffer dogs and searching every area of the ship, concentrating on the crew cabins and other crew areas. They sometimes came up empty, but often they would find drugs. It was mostly marijuana in those days stuffed in the bathroom's water tanks, sometimes in the engine room, and under the beds in the crew cabins. If they could somehow pin it on the person, he or she would be arrested immediately and taken off of the ship. I remember one waiter who had just started on the ship and he was getting off in Miami, when there were dogs in the terminal checking everyone who was getting off the ship, as he passed one of the dogs they started sniffing and sat down next to him, when the officer checked him they found small packets of cocaine in his shoes, he was handcuffed and taken away.

CHAPTER 15

Rescue at Sea

Life on a cruise ship is like working for a large hotel and living in a small village. We must carry everything on board to be self-sufficient, whether it's a part to fix the engine or some medicine that the doctor needs to stop a toothache. However, there comes a time when we need some outside help, and when this happens, we call the U.S. Coast Guard.

We had been at sea for two days in very rough weather, and there were many seasick passengers and crew. It didn't seem as if the weather was getting any better. There was a crosswind blowing at 45 miles an hour, and the sea waves were anywhere from 15 to 20 feet high. The ship would rise on a wave and then crash down at the bottom. It was moaning and creaking with every move, and as it hit the bottom of each wave, it would shudder and shake, and creaks and cracks could be heard as the wooden interior moved against the iron hull. I had been working on ships for several years and knew that the ship could handle it. I felt confident that we were reasonably safe; however, everyone always had to be careful moving around in order to make sure everything was tied down. It was also important to watch one's step if walking up or down stairs. With one movement of the ship, passengers or crew members could find themselves at the bottom of the stairs.

Safety is always a concern on the ship, but never so much as when it is in the middle of bad weather. Every department, from those who worked in the engine room to the kitchen staff, had a responsibility for securing their area to make it safe. The gift shop would remove all glass and china from the display windows, dismantle displays that might fall, and lay them on the ground. The restaurant and kitchen would make sure all of their plates and glasses were put into cabinets and racks that were closed up and sometimes wrapped with plastic wrap. Some equipment had brakes and a way to secure it to the floor, while some equipment had chains that could be attached to a wall so it would not move. The bad weather is one of the reasons that the tables in the restaurants are bolted to the floor.

It was around 8:00 p.m. on the second day of the terrible weather when I heard something was not right in the engine room. I saw the staff captain, the hotel manager, and the ship's doctor rushing down the back stairs towards the engine room, and they had concerned looks on their faces. It wasn't long after that when we heard that a young sailor, in his first year on the ship working in the engine room, had his leg crushed by a piece of machinery. He was losing a lot of blood as the doctor tried to stabilize him, out it was obvious that he needed to be taken care of in a hospital. If they were going to save his life, time was of the essence. The captain was on the bridge taking care of the ship during the bad weather. By that time, he had been there for 16 hours without rest, and the whole time he was kept apprised of the situation 18 decks below in the engine room. The doctor called the bridge on his radio and told the captain that he needed to get the crew member to a hospital as soon as possible. The captain immediately placed a call on the emergency radio to the Coast Guard explaining the situation. He gave them his position at sea and the direction the ship was heading, along with the ship's speed. We were about 100 miles off of the Florida coast, and the Coast Guard asked the captain to change course towards the coastline at which point they would send out a rescue crew. With the information they had, it would be about three hours before they would likely be able to get to the ship. In the meantime, the crew member was removed from the engine room to the ship's infirmary, and the ship's doctor was on the radio talking to a surgeon in Miami, trying his best to do whatever possible until the Coast Guard showed up.

Outside the aft end of the ship, some of the crew were removing deck chairs and whatever they could to clear the deck to make it easier for the Coast Guard to work when they arrived. This was back in the 1980s before cruise ships had helipads, which many of the new ships currently have.

Three hours passed quickly. It was around midnight when I went up on deck to watch the operation. Passengers were also gathering on the deck above me they were curious to see want was going on. It was dark with no moonlight, and no stars were visible. The wind was howling, and the rain was falling; the ship was bobbing up and down and from side to side with the waves still around 15 feet high. I couldn't imagine how they were going to remove the crew member from the ship.

A couple of moments later, I could just hear the sound of the blades in the distance. The Coast Guard helicopter was getting closer and its searchlight was dancing around the black ocean against the whitewash of the waves.

Just below me, a large heavy door opened, and the ship's doctor and nurse, along with some of the engine crew, pushed their way through the door carrying a collapsible stretcher with the sailor lying on it. He was wrapped up so well, I could just make out his face. His eyes were open and he looked scared. As they battled with the wind and rain, the Coast Guard helicopter moved slowly into position, hovering about 20 feet from the back deck of the ship. The pilot was watching straight ahead. He had a difficult time because the ship was rising and falling with the waves, and the rain and wind was hitting against the helicopter windows. At the side of the helicopter there were two men kneeling in an open door with a basket on a cable, waiting to drop it on the ship's desk when the pilot was ready to give the order.

A couple of times, the helicopter had to back away and approach the ship again. I found out after from the ship's captain that on the third attempt, the helicopter pilot said that if he couldn't get it close and steady enough, that they would have to leave. Luckily, though, on the third attempt, the pilot gave the order and one of the Coast Guard, along with the basket, was lowered to the ship's deck. At the same time, the crew with the doctor moved into position just below the helicopter, and within a couple of seconds, they removed the sailor from the stretcher to the basket. The doctor gave the Coast Guard some papers and then they were both hoisted up to the helicopter. Before they reached the open door, the pilot turned the helicopter out towards the sea and away from the ship. Soon, they disappeared into the darkness. The entire operation took about 10 minutes.

***

The next day, the captain announced over the PA system that the sailor was doing well and that they were able to save his leg. There were two other times in my career when the Coast Guard was called out to the ship—one was for a passenger, and the other for the hotel manager. Both had heart attacks and needed to get to a hospital, but neither of them were as dramatic as the experience with the sailor.

There were a couple of other times we had to rescue people from the sea. Early in the 1980s, there was a mass of people leaving Cuba and Haiti on small rafts, trying to reach the Florida Coast. I remember on one occasion we were on our way back to Miami. It was a beautiful day. The sky was blue, and the sea was calm like a sheet of glass. It was around 2:00 p.m. and most of us were just finishing up lunch when the captain spotted a small raft a couple of miles ahead of the ship. We were about 350 miles from the Florida coast in the Gulf Stream. As we got closer, we could see a small, homemade, wooden raft made from driftwood, and a sail made of old sheets. There looked to be about 15 people on the raft, which measured about 8 feet by 10 feet. It was about the size of a small bedroom.

There was not much movement on the raft, and at first the captain thought that everyone on the raft was dead, but as he got closer, he did see some movement. He slowed the ship down and came closer to the raft. He lowered some steps from a deck close to the ocean, and some of the officers and crew went down the steps. One by one, they carried everyone onto the ship and straight to the infirmary where the ship's doctor was waiting. They were completely dehydrated, their clothes were torn, and they all had sun stroke. A couple of them were rambling on in Spanish, not making much sense, although the doctor was from Spain. He made out that they were all from Haiti and had left there a week prior. It was surprising that anyone was still alive, if only barely. The doctor immediately put them on a drip to re-hydrate them, and the next day they were all looking better, yet still not able to eat as their lips were badly burned and cracked from the sun and salt.

When we arrived in Miami, the Immigration officers were waiting for us as the captain had informed them two days earlier that we had picked up the people. He wanted to make sure we were not breaking any laws, so he had to notify them. They moved them all to a hospital in Miami. It was later on when I found out that as soon as they were all well enough to travel, they were to be sent back to Haiti. It seemed probable that it wouldn't be long before they tried it again.

Of the thousands of people who fled Haiti and Cuba to find their freedom, hundreds did not make it. Some died of dehydration, sunstroke, and sunburn, while some tried to drink sea water, only to get stomach problems, which brought on sickness, diarrhea, and more dehydration. Most would try to get into the Gulf Stream which would take them up along the coast of Florida, but they would only find that they would be swept up by the current and taken back out into the Atlantic, never to been seen again. Some would end up in the ocean because their rafts would get broken up in the waves, and while trying to swim ashore, they would be attacked by sharks.

Every month we would practice a rescue for Man Overboard. Usually on a calm day at sea, the captain would get the passengers involved so that they not only could see how it was done, but also to make them aware that it was a drill and not a real situation. We would throw over a full size dummy, and the captain would say it was the cruise director. The ship's horn would blow one long blast; this was the signal for Man Overboard and certain crew members had different duties to deal with the situation. The ship would immediately turn in a circular pattern and return to the exact position where the person went overboard. A small boat would be lowered to the ocean and a small crew would head in the direction of the dummy to pick it up and return it to the ship. The whole exercise would take about an hour, at which time, the passengers would be let in on the secret that it was not actually the cruise director. He was the one making the announcements from the bridge.

Doing a drill like this in good weather and in daylight was one thing, but unfortunately, most real situations of this nature happen at night and in rougher weather. I remember a few occasions while I was sleeping when I was woken up by the ship's horn. Knowing the signal, I would get dressed and go up on deck to watch. At the back of the boat the only thing that could be seen was the wake from the ship as it was turning in a circle. The hotel manager would be woken up and his job was to talk to the person who raised the alarm. Usually they would say that they saw someone jump or fall over the rail, then they would try to do a head count of all of the passengers and crew to see if anyone was missing.

The captain would notify the Coast Guard, and they would send out a search party. Any ships in the area would also be notified, and if they were near enough, it was their duty to join in the search. I can say that on all those occasions, nobody was ever found. There are too many variables, including how long they would last in the water, sharks, how far they would drift, if they took in a lot of water after they jumped, and the fact that they would most likely drown in a couple of minutes. If they hit the side of the ship on the way down, the 75 foot drop could knock anyone out and cause that person to immediately sink, depending where the original jump occurred. People could also be sucked into the big propellers and be turned into mince meat, and that would be the end of that.

CHAPTER 16

Food, Food, and More Food

Food plays a big part on any cruise ship just as much today as it did twenty years ago. In fact, cruise ships have changed according to the trends and demands of the passengers. No longer must they stand in long lines waiting for the doors to open into the restaurant, then rush to their seats and hope their waiter doesn't give them a strange look for being late. No longer do they have to decide between early or late seating on some cruise ships, and if they get hungry in the middle of the night, they can call for room service or take a walk on deck and find some snacks.

It has always amazed me how people think they must go on a starvation diet before taking a cruise so they have plenty of room to eat all they can. In fact, the complete opposite applies.

An example of this is how on one cruise, I saw a passenger who seemed very upset. When I asked if everything was okay, his wife explained to me as she laughed that her husband decided a month earlier that he was going on a strict diet before the cruise so he could eat everything in sight while on the ship. However, what he didn't realize was that as he dieted and restricted himself, his stomach got smaller, so it didn't need as much. When he was on the cruise four weeks later, he could not eat as much as he wanted.

However one looks at it, there is no way anyone can eat all the food that is available, although I have seen many people try.

When I started in the cruise business, there was one dining room with two sittings—one early and one late. Passengers had to decide at the beginning of the cruise which one to pick. Early seating was around 6:00 p.m., and late was around 8.30 p.m. Some cruise ships would ask passengers when they booked the cruise, and some would wait until they were boarding the first day. Then there was a choice at breakfast and lunch. There was the regular eating in the main dining room or a light breakfast and limited lunch on the open deck, usually beside the pool, in an area called the pool deck or sun deck. Then, of course, there was the midnight buffet every night, and when passengers would ask the classic question, " What time is the midnight buffet?" crew members would reply, "Why, midnight, of course." Someone always asked that question every cruise, and it became a classic joke among the crew. Of course, times have changed and cruise ships have several restaurants serving different cuisine all day long. There are standard restaurants, specialty restaurants that often require reservations, as well as pizza style family dining and room service that usually are open 24 hours, and some sort of buffet by the pool all day long. Some even have their own ice cream parlors and pub grub. The sky's the limit when it comes to food, and what the passengers ask for, the cruise line does its best to make happen. They are always looking for the next trend in food service.

The quality has also improved over the years. The cruise lines realize they must hire really talented chefs and look to purchase better products than they did years ago. The competition is so tough that the cruise ship that stays ahead of every other ship will win.

The logistics of shopping for and delivering all of the food and beverages to each ship every week can be a nightmare. Each cruise line will have an entire department to take care of this—a purchasing department. They are responsible for getting all of the food and beverages to each ship, whether it may be in Miami or Milan, and negotiating the best prices for everything. I remember on one occasion I was on a ship going to Ocho Rios, Jamaica and we were to pick up a container on the dock which was shipped earlier that week with, among other things, six hundred pounds of lobster tails. We had Caribbean lobster tails on the menu that night. When we arrived and all of the passengers got off, myself and the chef went looking for the container, and when we found it, it was empty; we asked the Customs officer where the contents was, and he told us that one of our sister ships had been there the day before and they took it all. We called the office in a panic to let them know we did not know what to do. They could not get us the lobster on time before the ship sailed that night. I was the dining room manager at the time, and the chef and I went through all of the freezers and fridges.

The chef said there were enough lobster tails for the first seating (around 600 people) if the waiters did not sell too much, and he found some frozen lobster meat which could do for about one hundred people on the second seating. Within an instant we looked at each other, and at that moment we knew what each one of us was thinking. We went to the hotel manager and told him our plan. We would tell the waiters to suggest other items on the menu and avoid the lobster unless the guest ordered it. Then, after the first seating, we would send all of the lobster shells through the dishwasher, air dry them, and send them to the kitchen. The chef would fill the shells with the lobster meat and broil them in the oven for the second seating. The hotel manager agreed, saying facetiously how he hadn't heard the plan, but to do what we had to do. Later that night everyone who ordered lobster was served lobster and no one was the wiser. We pulled it off. Needless to say, the head office was impressed, but they made sure nothing of the sort would ever happen again.

***

An average cruise ship uses a huge amount of supplies every week. These include: 20,000 pounds of flour, 30,000 pounds of sugar, 10,000 eggs, 5,000 pounds of butter, 12,000 gallons of milk, 10,000 pounds of beef, 15,000 pounds of fish, 600 pounds of fresh shrimp, 12,000 pounds of bacon, 5,000 pounds of lobster, 40 pounds of mixed green lettuce, 60 pounds of romaine lettuce, 200 pounds each of carrots, celery, and onions, 500 pounds of potatoes, 50 pounds of cabbage, 100 pounds each of apples, pears, oranges, and melons, as well as 70 pounds of bananas, 60 pounds of red and green grapes, 900 gallons of coffee, 1,000 gallons of iced tea, 400 pounds of cooking chocolate, 50,000 bottles of water, 200,000 bottles of beer, 35,000 bottles of wine, 10,000 bottles of mixed spirits, and 60,000 bottles of soda.

The weekly gala buffet always took around 400 hours to put together. Every department in the kitchen gets their chance to pull out all the stops and be very creative. The gala buffet usually takes place on one of the last nights of the cruise. There were twelve 300-pound blocks of ice carved into swans, mermaids, dolphins, etc., as well as large displays of salmon, pork, beef, and chicken. A large ice sculpture of a bowl filled to the brim with shrimp, another big display on a glass mirror of lobster, and around 40 different cakes and desserts. The artistry that came out of the small kitchen every week from the many talented chefs was mind-blowing.

With over thirty different nationalities on board, there is always a great variety of food cooked on the ship. With cooks from Asia, Europe, and many other countries to cook for the crew, there is always a way to make crew members happy by providing some good home cooking for them. It's also a great way for everyone to be exposed to the many different styles of food and tastes from around the world.

When walking down a corridor in the crew area, one could travel through Asia, and then there are great smells of curry coming from the Indian rooms, while a little further on, there may be smells of Thai and Filipino food, and then when stepping into the laundry, one can see a Chinese cook making some breakfast for his crew at 3:00 a.m. I must say I had a glorious experience while I was on board, tasting foods from all over the world.

We all ate well on the ship, and when our sister ship would meet up with us every two weeks in San Juan the dining room manager's would take it in turns to go and visit the other ship and the chef would cook an amazing meal for us, it became a competition to see see which chef could come up with the best meal to see if they could out do each other. When I was a waiter on the Song of Norway, we would go over to the Sun Viking between dinner seatings to help the other waiter get ready for the second seating and the next time we met they would come over and help us it was also a great way to chat with friends, unfortunately with all the security that's something you can't do today sadly.

One of our dining room managers, Roberto from Italy, loved to cook. Nearly every night, he would cook a large bowl of pasta for the head waiters and the entire dining room staff. After normal service, when dinner was over for our guests, he would disappear into the kitchen and load up one of the large boiling pots with about 20 pounds of pasta, and while it sat on the stove, he would make his sauce. He used a couple of large tins of tomatoes, along with garlic, onions, oregano, red pepper, and cheese, before bringing it into the dining room, mixing it all together, and serving it to the staff. With a few bottles of Jordan wine and some crunchy bread, we were living la dolce vita, the sweet life in Italian.

I remember one night when Roberto told us not to order food since he was making his special pasta that night; we were all waiting longer than usual, unsure why he was taking so long. I decided to go and check on him, and when I entered the kitchen, I saw him down on his knees trying to gather all the pasta up that was on the ground. Apparently one of the large pots tipped over and the pasta and water spilled out all over the floor. I laughed, then helped him gather all the pasta up, wash it off, and put it back into the pot and bring it back to a boil. We brought it into the dining room along with the sauce and dished it out to the staff. No one was any the wiser what happened in the kitchen. Only he and I knew and we kept it our secret.

Roberto was also a big smoker, and many times he had a cigarette in the corner of his mouth as he would serve the pasta out of the large bowl. Several times, the ash would drop off of the end of his cigarette and fall into the pasta.

He would curse in Italian and just continue to mix it up and portion it out onto the next waiter's plate who was standing in line. Everyone enjoyed his cooking and always looked forward to his meals. I'm sure Roberto is cooking up a storm in Heaven. He was a very special person and a good friend of mine; I miss him every day.

***

One day, Slavko, one of our head waiters, met some officers from a Russian cruise ship. He struck up a conversation with them and invited them back to our ship for lunch; they had such a good time that we met up with them every week. We would take it in turns—one week they would come over to our ship, the next we would go over to theirs for lunch. They would bring over large tins of Beluga caviar and Russian vodka and we asked them what we could bring them. They wanted American jeans, Levis, as they were not allowed to dock in any American port, and for some reason, they loved jeans and could not buy them in Russia. So, when we were in Miami, we would buy up a load of jeans and trade them for the caviar. They were so excited to get the jeans, but I think we got the better end of the deal.

***

Back in my early cruise ship years, when I was the captain's waiter, I had a busboy who worked with me. His name was Chong, and he was from South Korea. He was a jovial type, but there was one thing he insisted I order for him every morning, and that was smoked salmon, cream cheese, and bagels. I remember one morning I forgot and he was so upset the whole day that he made me pick up my own china and silverware from the kitchen. I made sure I didn't forget ever again.

We didn't realize back then how good we had it. Every night, we would eat smoked salmon, steaks, lobster, coq au vin, and pretty much whatever we wanted. Sometimes the chef would make us something special, and we would bring the best wine and champagne to our table every night.

One day we were in Martinique and there was a great French shop selling the most amazing cheeses, imported from France. Roberto and I bought an extensive selection of cheeses and French bread. We spent about $300, and that was a lot back in 1982. We returned to the ship and couldn't wait to have a great meal of cheese and wine for dinner. Roberto and I, along with his assistant and two other head waiters, had the best meal we'd ever had, but we couldn't finish the cheese, so we asked the waiter to wrap it up and put it into a fridge that was next to a waiter's side stand in the dining room, and we would enjoy another night of the cheese.

The very next night, we purposely didn't order any food because we were going to enjoy the cheese again. We all sat down ready for another great dinner, but when the waiter went to get the cheese from the fridge, it was gone. The fridge was empty. Roberto was so mad that he was thumping his fists on the table. One of the head waiters, Joe, said he was checking the dining room after lunch and he smelled something. When he opened the fridge, he thought he cheese had gone bad, so he threw it in the garbage. I thought Roberto was going to strangle him. Needless to say, we didn't have any dinner that night.

On another night, Tony from Ireland, a good buddy of mine, was the waiter on the head waiter's table. It was one of his duties to collect food for the dining room manager and head waiters each night. When we all sat down to eat, I noticed there was no food put aside for us. Serge from France was the dining room manager, and he was very picky about his food. Tony either had forgotten to collect our food or the food was stolen by the other waiters. The latter was most likely; however, when Tony realized what had happened, he said, "Guys, I have prepared a very special meal for you all tonight." He rushed back into the kitchen, and with the help of one of the cooks, he collected some ingredients and quickly put together a delicious meal. When he brought it to the table, everyone was very impressed and enjoyed the whole meal. Serge said it was one of the best meals he ever had.

I was on a ship that sailed on the last day from Freeport in the Bahamas back to Port Canaveral; it was a short trip so sometime during the night the ship would stop and just drift to save fuel and also if we kept going we would arrive to early at Cape Canaveral, so the hotel manager Melvin who liked to fish off the back of the ship, would go up every week and try to fish the only problem was he was 40 feet from the water line so any fish he caught would drop off the line before he could get it into the boat, after a few weeks he decided to try and fish for sharks, he bought some strong lines and big hooks in Miami, then he would ask the chef for some blood and scraps from the butcher, putting it into a big bucket he would go up on deck and start by pouring some of the blood overboard it didn't take long for the sharks to start circling the ship, one particular night he managed to hook one and it took several of us about an hour to wrestle with the big shark and finally got it on board, Melvin stood proudly beside the fish which was taller that him and Melvin was over 6ft 2in himself as the ships photographer took several photos of both of them, the next day the chef cut up and cooked the shark and we all have a great meal that day.

As I mentioned earlier, one of the great things about working on the cruise ship is not only the people, but the food. I remember on one occasion when I was a dining room manager, I was invited to dine with the Chinese in the laundry room. This was a very special event, as it wasn't every day that anyone would have the privilege to dine with them in the laundry. This was something I was looking forward to, and I felt it was very special that they had asked me to join them. I put on my white uniform and proceeded down to the laundry room where I was met by the chief. He looked about thirty, a small man with a bald head, pale skin, and a long mustache. He was wearing a white robe like a dressing gown and some flip-flops on his feet. Everyone seemed to be waiting for him to make a move. Later, I found out he was nearly sixty. He greeted me with a bow and directed me to a table that was set up for about twenty people. We had a drink of sake and then the food arrived. I couldn't count how many dishes there were, but there were a lot. The food was amazing. There were several dishes from different regions of China. It was one of the best meals I ever had on a ship. Not only was I feeling very special that they invited me, but they too were very excited that I came down to join them for a meal. It was an exceptional experience, and one I will never forget.

CHAPTER 17

Fire at Sea

It's one of the most frightening experiences that can happen at sea, and even though the ship is surrounded by water, a fire on a ship can quickly get out of hand and the ship can go down. However, a well-trained captain and crew and a quick response can save many lives.

Safety is number one on a cruise ship, and every person on the crew is highly trained when it comes to fire fighting and prevention. Every week the crew has a full fire and lifeboat drill.

The drills always took place when we were in port, and usually after most of the passengers were ashore. The captain would blow seven short blasts, followed by one long blast on the ship's whistle. This was the signal for the entire crew to go and put on their life jackets and proceed to their emergency stations. Everyone had a designated area. In the fourteen years that I was at sea, I manned almost every station, except for the captain's. One station involved standing outside of the elevators and directing passengers p the stairs to the lifeboats. Another was to run down a orridor of passenger cabins, banging on all doors to tell assengers to grab their life jackets and proceed to their mergency stations. Yet another was to go straight to the ifeboats or life rafts and start getting them ready just in ase the captain gave the order to abandon ship. Once veryone was at their emergency stations, we would wait bout 20 minutes before the captain blew one long blast on he ship's whistle, followed by an announcement to abandon hip. All passengers and crew then proceeded to their ifeboat and life raft stations.

We would all proceed to the lifeboat deck, and some f the crew would already be there and have the boats owered to the deck, ready for disembarkation. A handful of s would climb into the lifeboats and rafts, and then they vould be lowered down to the water level and we would o a small circle around the harbor and return up the side f the ship. This not only was a way to make sure the crew new what to do in case of an emergency, but also a good pportunity to make sure all of the equipment was working roperly. Every couple of months, the supplies in each feboat and raft would be replaced. There was dried food ke crackers, about two gallons of water for each person on ach lifeboat, and to make sure it was ready to use, even the ares would be tested and changed out.

This routine was a pain for most of us, eating into ur valuable nap time; however, it was important and nandatory by the US Coast Guard. None of us expected we vould ever have to go through an actual emergency.

It's difficult to put a fire out, especially if it gets out of control quickly.

I had been working on ships for over 12 years with no actual emergencies except for two occasions both within the same year of each other.

One night we were sailing toward the Panama Canal. We had just started the first seating in the dining room and everything was going well. It was a beautiful night with calm seas and a full moon dancing on the horizon. We were getting all of the entrées out of the kitchen when I noticed what seemed to be an abnormally large amount of smoke. When I asked the chef, he said one of his exhaust fans over the grill was not working and that was causing more smoke in the kitchen than normal. As we were starting the second seating, one of the waiters came over and pulled me aside to tell me there was a fire in the kitchen. I walked quickly to the kitchen, where I was greeted with a kitchen full of smoke and the grill was in flames while a couple of chefs were trying to put it out. The chef was calling the bridge for help, and within minutes, a group of firefighters arrived in full fire gear with extinguishers. It took them about thirty minutes to put the fire out and another thirty minutes to clean the grill and kitchen before we could resume service.

I and my head waiters went around to all of the guests in the dining room. By this time they knew that there had been a fire. Some had left the restaurant, but most stayed. We explained to them we would be back in service in an hour and then could serve them. We did resume service, and everyone enjoyed their dinner. It may have had something to do with the free wine we gave everyone that night.

The other occasion was more serious. It was late at night off the coast of Alaska. It was 2:30 a.m. on a Tuesday morning when I awoke to the sound of the emergency alarms ringing and an announcement from the bridge for all passengers and crew to make their way to the lifeboats. I knew it was the real thing. We had just left Juneau, the capital of Alaska, at 10:00 p.m. the previous night, and we were on our way to Sitka, a small fishing village further north up the coast. It was the last night at sea for most of our passengers. About half of the passengers would disembark while there and fly back to the States. The other half would return with the ship as it made its way to Vancouver.

It took me a second or two before I jumped out of bed and pulled on a pair of long trousers and a T-shirt. As I was shoving my feet into my shoes, I remembered we were in Alaska, so I put on an extra pullover and grabbed my life jacket. I took a last look around my cabin to see if there was something I could take, as I had a feeling there was the possibility I would not get to see my cabin again. I quickly grabbed my wallet and watch and proceeded out of my cabin and down a long corridor which was pitch black except for reflective tape along the floor. There were no usual creaks and moans or vibrations from the big engines. Instead, there was an eerie silence and I could tell the ship was listing to one side. As I got to the top of the stairs—eight decks up—I pushed open the doors to the boat deck and the cold Alaskan air hit my face like tiny stabbing knives. There were many passengers gathering on the boat deck and they were remarkably calm. I think it was because they had just woken up, so the full impact of what was happening had not yet hit them.

It tends to be much easier to get everyone from their cabins up to the lifeboat deck at night when they are all already in their cabins than when it is earlier in the day and there are passengers all over the ship. There is more of a chance that there will be panic and confusion if people are coming from all over.

Ten decks below, the firefighting crew was in the boiler room fighting a fire that started by an electric panel, behind a wall, next to the boiler room. They spent the next three hours fighting the fire; meanwhile, up on deck, the crew were handing out blankets to all of the passengers to keep them warm. Along with the cold Alaskan air, most of the elderly passengers were suffering from shock, which also lowers body temperature.

It was a clear night. The air was still, and I could see the full moon and stars in the sky, but there was no land in sight. When I looked over the side, I could see a calm sea with tiny ripples reflecting the moon. The captain had sent out the International Emergency Signal for help and had received a signal from another cruise ship about four hours away. They immediately changed their course to proceed in our direction. Three hours after the first signal to proceed to the lifeboats, the captain received a message from the boiler room that they were losing the battle with the fire and that the chief engineer said it didn't look good and how we might have to abandon the ship soon. The captain thought for a moment, and then the chief engineer called the captain on the radio again to say they were in control; the fire was out, and the ship, although listing and with no power, was safe. At this time, the captain made the announcement over the PA system that it was safe to return to the cabins. Not knowing exactly what had taken place, the passengers descended the stairs back to their cabins, relieved to get out of the cold night air. Again, they moved quietly and without panic.

Some passengers returned to their cabins, while others went to the ballroom. I was sitting in the middle of the dining room with the chef when an elderly couple came into the room and asked us what time breakfast was scheduled. The chef and I burst out laughing.

Some guests stayed up on deck. All were confused and tired. They began to hear what had happened in the boiler room, and as the fire had been extinguished and the crew were assessing the damage, the captain knew the ship was unstable. We still had no power to run the air conditioning, and we still only had emergencies light from the batteries. We didn't even have the power to move the ship, The captain was in touch with the other cruise ship in the area that was heading closer to us and would reach us in the next hour. The captain explained that he would have to move all of our passengers over to the other ship and that they would continue on to Sitka where they would all disembark and board buses which would take them to Anchorage where they would catch flights back to their homes.

It was 8:00 a.m. the following morning when the other cruise ship arrived. The passengers were quickly moved to the other ship. A couple of our crew went with them. The cruise director and a couple of his staff assisted the passengers; meanwhile, the rest of the crew waited for two tugboats to arrive from Juneau and tow us to the nearest port which was a small town in Alaska called Whittier. It took about another four hours before the tugboats reached us and then another ten hours to tow us to Whittier. It was in Whittier where a team of insurance people, along with some executives from our head office, arrived to assess the damage. While that was happening, we had a couple of days in Whittier to roam around and get to know the locals. It was a small town population of around 200 people, and there was a bar, restaurant, and post office, as well as a small grocery store and a hospital. One man owned the bar, restaurant, and store. There was no gas station as there was only one road a half mile long through the town. At one end was the pier where we were and the other end was the train station, with one track. Once a week, a train would come from Anchorage and drop off or take on a few passengers. There was a tunnel at the end of town and that was the only way in and out of Whittier, not counting the sea. The local's said, "If you wanted to hide the president of the United States for safety, this would be the perfect place." On night on the ship we all woke up as the ship tilted about another 10 degrees at the pier, we were all so scared we all left the ship and stood on the pier in the middle of the night no-one wanted to go back on board we all stood there in the freezing cold. The next few days our company was able to get us to Anchorage and then fly home.

CHAPTER 18

The American Adventure

One year I returned from my vacation and when I reported to the office in Cape Canaveral, the operations manager asked me if I like to go to Italy and bring a new ship to Miami. At first, I was excited. He explained that our company had acquired the food and beverage concession for a new venture with a new company in connection with the Italian Line, Costa Cruise Line. The ship was called the American Adventure and would sail a one-week cruise out of Miami geared towards families and kids, to which I replied, "I'm in."

I worked in the office for the next four weeks, figuring out how many crew members we would need, how to set up the dining rooms, what kinds of theme nights there would be, dining room stations, and for the first time in the industry, the passengers would pay their tips upfront, so I had to work out how to divide up the tips on board. When I arrived in Genoa, Italy, I took a train ride to La Spezia on the coast to join the ship in wet dock. The ship was being refurbished; they had amazing facilities for the kids, great big playrooms, even including a Cinderella themed midnight buffet for the kids which started at 8:00 p.m. and had every kind of chocolate and candy imaginable.

During dry dock, a group of us would meet every night at the gangway around 7:00 p.m. and go ashore for an Italian dinner. We would walk down to the end of the pier where we found a great restaurant run by a typical Italian family. The father was in the back cooking, mother and daughter out front serving the guests, and grandmother watching the till. After a few nights of confusion, we would not even look at the menu's; they would just bring us several courses and a couple of bottles of wine and we would happily pay at the end of the night. Typical fare was some kind of appetizer, crostini, roast tomato bruschetta, Caprese salad with fresh mozzarella, tomatoes, fresh basil, and a drizzle of aged balsamic vinegar and locally made prosciutto, as well as some wine followed by some variety of pastas, more wine, pizzas and a meat dish, even more wine, sometimes a dessert or some local cheeses and freshly baked bread, along with an espresso, and some sambuca. We all ate like kings, fat and happy, as we returned to the ship to sleep it off.

On our last day and during our last meal in La Spezia, it seemed like we were presented with more food than we could consume and farewells from the owners of the restaurant. They had tears in their eyes. We were not sure if they were going to miss us or our money, maybe a bit of both.

We loaded up the ship with all of the supplies we would need for the crossing, which would be six days and nights across the Atlantic. We had several extra tradespeople to finish working on the ship during the crossing.

One stipulation was that we had to serve the Italian offic and crew wine with their meals. It was in their contracts, so loaded up with boxes of Italian wine for our journey, but bef got out of the Mediterranean one days later, we had already r of wine. A quick call and a stop in Gibraltar in the middle of night allowed us to load up with more wine for the crossing. our trip, after about three days at sea, I got a call from the Pu Office that they wanted me to help them with their computer system. I knew a little about computers, but not a lot, so I went over to see if I could help. As I met the chief p he told me they couldn't open their computer system because didn't know the passwords. I sat down to think and consider the ship was from Italy, so I told them to try typing "Italy," w they did, but it didn't work. I then told them to try typing "N and they did that, too, but again, it didn't work, I asked them did the ship sail before we took it over, and someone said, "A believe." I said to try that, and at that moment all of the com lit up and started re-booting. They were once again all syster

***

Halfway across the Atlantic, I went up on deck with my radio to get some fresh air and see if I could find a station to listen to, but there was complete silence on the FM and

SW bands. It was at that moment when I realized how far we were from any land and civilization.

Several days later, we arrived safely in Miami. The seas were calm as we were traveling in the summer and across the lower half of the Atlantic all the way. We did a lot of training during the crossing and every day we would practice boat drills over and over so we could all do it blindfolded; they were several carpenters, fitters, and painters on board finishing up the ship so we would be ready to sail after a week in Miami. We would have to go through a full safety drill with the U.S. Coast Guard before we would be given permission to sail with passengers the following Saturday.

After the first week's cruise, I got a call from the purser to collect the tips from the first cruise, so I went over to pick them up; he handed me a big heavy canvas bag and a slip for me to sign. My jaw dropped when I saw I was signing a receipt for $80,000. When I dragged it back to my cabin, I immediately called the shoreside office and asked them to send me a safe next time we came to Miami. It was a lot of money to keep even for one night before I would pay everyone the next day. Roberto, one of my head waiters, and myself were well versed in computers, and we both had new laptops. This was back in the early 1990s when they were expensive. We used a software called Microsoft Access to set up a system to pay everyone in the dining room quickly; it was so good that the head housekeeper asked me if we would do the same for him and his housekeeping staff, which we did.

***

During each cruise, we would have several theme nights where the head waiters would dress up. On night one, it was hero night, and they would dress up as Batman and Robin, Superman and Spiderman. They would lift Superman on their shoulders and fly through the dining room. The kids would go crazy. I think my head waiters had more fun than the kids. Another evening, it was movie night, and they would dress up as Groucho and Harpo Marx, Charlie Chaplin, Keystone Cops, and Coco the Clown. Another night they would dress up as cowboys and chase each other around the dining room shooting at each other. I remember looking at the kids' faces as they lit up while watching the whole show. It was the highlight of their cruise.

After several months on board, we were anchored off a small private island near the coast of Punta Cana in the Dominican Republic, when I got a call from the bridge. It was from the head office in Miami. They wanted me to leave the ship before it sailed at 5:00 p.m. to go to a ship in Alaska. They had to fire the dining room manager and needed a replacement immediately. I would be replaced by another manager coming back from vacation at the end of the cruise. At this point in the day, it was 4:00 p.m., so I had to pack quickly and be ready by the gangway to meet the ship's agent so we could take a tender to the mainland. I quickly shoved all of my clothes into my case when I realized I had about $8,000 in cash, so I put it into a small gym bag with dirty socks and underwear and a few T-shirts and headed to the gangway. The agent and I took the tender to Punta Cana, and from there I flew in a small plane to Puerto Rico where I got another flight to Miami.

I was sitting in the plane in Puerto Rico waiting for them to close the doors when I realized I hadn't identified my small gym bag, so I started to panic. I called the hostess over and explained to her that I left a bag behind in the airport. She said not to worry, if the tag was on the bag, I would be reunited with it in Miami. I wasn't so sure. I tried to keep calm the whole trip as I had visions of someone in Customs opening my bag and taking all my cash. We arrived in Miami about an hour and a half later that night, and as I waited for my second bag, it never came off of the conveyer belt. I went to report it missing and was told there were five more flights from Puerto Rico that night and it should be on one of them. I gave them the details, including the color of the bag and the clothes in it, but never mentioned the $8,000. They asked for my hotel information and said they would send it to the hotel as soon as they found it.

I grabbed a taxi at the airport, and it dropped me off at the Marriott Hotel in Miami. While checking in, I told the receptionist I was expecting a bag from the airport and she said she would call my room as soon as they received it. I thanked her and made my way to my room.

It was a long night, I called down from my room several times to check if my bag was delivered and the answer was always the same—they hadn't received anything. It was after midnight and I knew there were no more flights coming from Puerto Rico, so I planned to check again in the morning.

The next morning, I was to fly to Alaska. I was having breakfast in the hotel dining room, but I was not hungry because I had a sinking feeling in my stomach, thinking the money was gone and that I would never see it again. It depressed me to think of how long it would take me to make it back again, when over the intercom I heard my name mentioned. I rushed over to the reception desk and there was a driver from the airport with my bag in his hand; I showed him my identification, and he handed it to me. I immediately ran up to my hotel room, emptied everything on to the bed, and along with my underwear, out fell the money. I quickly counted it and that morning I rushed over to my bank and deposited $8,000 in my account. I was finally ready to go to Alaska. I dodged a bullet that day.

During my time in Alaska, I got another call from the office. They wanted me to represent the company in court. A waiter was suing the company over money he felt he was owed from a ship I was on a year ago, so I had to again leave the ship and fly back to Miami. I appeared in court and made my statement under oath, and based on my statement, the judge dropped the case. Our company won. I went back to the office and the owner, Mr. Frazer, was thrilled and thanked me very much. He said his lawyer told him that my statement won the case.

Mr. Frazer called Eric, who was in charge of the entire crew, into his office and said to give me whatever I wanted, including if I wanted to go back on the ship or take some time off. I said I would like a few days off before returning to Alaska, and he gave me a week off, got me a car so I could drive home to Cape Canaveral for a week, and then get me a ticket to Alaska from Orlando for the following week. He stood up and shook my hand one more time. Eric ran out of his office and started making phone calls to arrange everything for me.

Not only did I help the company and save them a lot of money, but I also had a pleasant week's vacation.

I returned to the American Adventure several months later. On the captain's birthday, I tried to get him to come down to the dining room and have dinner with the passengers, but he was not one who liked to have a crowd around him. Instead, I got a bunch of waiters and a birthday cake with candles and took it up to his room where we all sang happy birthday in English and then Italian to him. By the end of the first year, the owners decided not to renew the lease on the ship. While it was a brilliant concept and a great idea, and many of these ships are what Disney uses today, I feel they were not making money. All of the adults were not spending money on board as everything was free for the kids. It was a sad day when we left the ship in Miami. The last four people who left the ship were the hotel manager, Kai, the food and beverage manager, Gerhard, the head waiter, Paulo, and myself, as we were the first four people to join the ship one year prior. At the end of the gangway, we all turned back to look up at the ship, and up on the bridge we could see the captain waving goodbye to us.

CHAPTER 19

My Last Cruise I

There were three last cruises. My first was when I met the love of my life, Meridith. I remember it like it was yesterday. The moment I met her, I said to myself, I am going to marry this girl one day.

It was a cruise, just like any other. I was working on Embarkation Day at our home port, Cape Canaveral, checking in all of the passengers for their dinner reservations.

Everything was going well, nothing unexpected. I was nearing the end of the reservations when I noticed a beautiful young woman walk into the room; she was stunning, around five foot six, with short, dark hair and a smile that could light up any room. She walked over to me and asked if it was too late to make dinner reservations; I felt like saying, "No, and you can sit at my table for dinner," but instead I said, "No, it's never too late."

She replied, "Oh, thank you, see there are six of us, my best friend and four others from the office. We all work for the cruise line."

"That's great," I said. "Which department do you work in? I have never seen you before."

"We all work in group sales; I work very close with corporate groups and often travel with them. However, this time we are all taking a cruise for fun and to relax." I handed her back the boarding passes with their table number.

"Thank you," I replied. "I will see you later for dinner, I hope. Have a great cruise.»

"Thank you," she said with a big smile, before turning and walking away.

That night in the dining room, I kept looking over at her table, and she looked beautiful.

At the beginning of every cruise we get a list from the office of all the passengers who are having an Anniversary, or Birthday or any special occasion and Meridith's birthday was on the list so later on that evening, I approached her table carrying a birthday cake. We all sang happy birthday to her, and after she blew out the candles, I leaned over to her and wished her a happy birthday.

Later that night while working the midnight buffet, Manuel, another head waiter, was busy checking out all of the single ladies who came into the buffet, trying to make a date with them for later. He was a very good-looking guy, full of confidence, and he had a great personality. It was no problem for him to have five or six girls lined up each cruise. Not only would they fall in love with his looks, but add to that his accent and the white officer's uniform with bars on his shoulders, and they were hooked.

It was approaching 1:00 a.m., the time to close the buffet, when in walked all of the girls from the office, including Meridith. They grabbed a few desserts and took a seat in the corner. Manuel and I sat across from them in the opposite corner. Manuel was talking to me, saying something about having it all arranged. He told me we would be meeting up with two girls later on—two sisters. He told them he would bring a friend along. I was not really listening to him; I was staring across the room at Meridith. Watching her every move, a couple of times she would look over our way and we would hear a few giggles coming from their table. Slowly, one by one, her friends left the table and did not return. When her last friend stood up, I told myself I needed to make my move then and there if I had any chance to be with her.

I stood up. Manuel put his hand on my arm and said, "Where are you going, buddy? I have everything arranged."

I pulled my arm away and replied, "Manuel, I appreciate it, but I have to go over and see if I can talk to this girl. She was glancing over here all night and now that he is alone, I must make my move."

Manuel was angry. He had come upon a problem—how was he going to separate the two sisters? He knew from experience that for him to get lucky he would have to get rid of one of the two, because together he would not get any action. "Sorry," I said, as I got up from my seat and crossed the room.

As I got to Meridith's table, I introduced myself and asked if I could join her.

She replied, "Sure, have a seat."

It was four o'clock when we both realized we had talked for three hours. It seemed more like ten minutes; we were having such a good time together. I asked her if she wanted to take a walk on deck and get some fresh air.

She replied, "Sure, you lead the way."

We both got up and headed towards the fire doors at the other end of the dining room, then up four flights of stairs, pushed open a door marked "Crew Only," and found ourselves on an open deck.

The breeze hit us as we walked towards the back of the ship. We stood for a while at the rail looking over the side; it was a clear night, a full moon was high above us off the starboard side. It was shimmering on the sea below as we gazed up at the stars and tried to identify some of them. Meridith turned to me and said, "I am feeling cold."

"Sorry," I said, as I removed my jacket and wrapped it around her bare shoulders. I put my arm around her, and she snuggled closer to me. We could feel the vibrations coming from the propellers below. As they churned up white waves, we would both follow each wave to see how far it would go until it disappeared into the darkness. We turned to look at each other, and her lips met mine. It was a gentle kiss at first, and then a longer, more open one. Both of our lips were salty from the sea spray. We didn't speak a word, just holding each other and thinking what a great ending it was to a great day.

We met every night on deck that cruise and talked, kissed, and even laid down together on one of the deck chairs. One night we fell asleep. I woke up first and watched the sun rise on the edge of the ocean. I was content and happy. I knew she was the one.

We never went to our own cabins the whole cruise; we had something special and didn't want to rush things.

I said goodbye to Meridith when we arrived back at our home port. She disappeared down the gangway. I found myself already missing her.

Meridith took several more cruises with me and for the ones she didn't, I would meet her for lunch in Cape Canaveral. When I arrived in the Bahamas, I would go out after dinner and find a public phone to call her. She would be wrapped up in bed and I would be outside, sometimes in the rain, but I was in love, so I didn't care. We would talk for hours; my monthly phone bill was always around six hundred dollars. I didn't care, though, as I would have paid a thousand dollars just to hear her voice.

Meridith came on a cruise a few months later to surprise me, and we cemented our relationship. It was the sweetest love making I had experienced; being in love is very special.

A couple of months later, I proposed to Meridith, and she said yes.

***

We were married on October 8, 1988. Both of us decided to leave the ship life behind and start our new adventure.

It was hard for me at first. I literally felt like a fish out of water.

At one point, the operations manager asked me to come back to the company. He told me that they were going to promote me to Assistant Food and Beverage Manager and train me to be the manager. It was tempting; however, I was excited about starting a new life with the woman I loved, so I said thanks, but no thanks.

Meridith and I bought a nice home in Florida near her parents and bought a puppy, I went on several interviews for jobs, but when they asked me what I was doing the last seven years, I would tell them with pride, I was working on a cruise ship. The problem was that my positions on the ship could not relate to any normal job on land. I finally got a job in a restaurant as a manager, earning a third of the money I made on the ship.

After three glorious years, Meridith and I split up. I was never home since I was working long hours, I might as well been on the ship at least I would make more money, and she was lonely. She went out with a couple of friends and met someone with whom she fell in love. Not long after that, we got divorced and went our separate ways. I was devastated, and I never got over it. I returned to the ships and got my old job back.

CHAPTER 20

My Last Cruise II

The second time I left the ships was something over which I had no control.

I was working for a food concessionaire and they supplied all of the food and beverage operations for their fleet of cruise ships. They had very old ships, but the nice thing was they had ships that went to so many different places like Alaska, South America, and through the Panama Canal. I got to see so many places, and it was exciting. However, it all came to an abrupt end one day.

I was on vacation and had just returned to work. I went over to the office in Miami and they said I was to join the two-day cruise out of Miami. The dining room manager was due for vacation and would I take over for him for six weeks. I said this was fine, but I had not worked on a two-day cruise before. We would leave Miami early in the evening around 4:00 p.m. to the Bahamas, stay overnight, and sail back the next day. It was an easy cruise; although, I wish it was the other way around and we could have stayed overnight in Miami.

It was an established fact when taking over for a dining room manager who was just going on vacation and then returning to the same ship that changes would not be made. It was easiest to keep things as they were as he would have set up everything his way and wanted to return to the ship the same way he left it.

I was not planning to change anything; however, one day I was working out the waiters' stations and side jobs when a young man from the Dominican Republic approached me and asked if he could have a word with me.

He said, "My name is Clarence. I have worked as the dining room cleaner on board for two years now, and I feel I have done a good job. Every time a new dining room manager comes to the ship, I ask him if he'll give me a chance as a busboy."

I replied, "As you're aware, I'm not supposed to change anything in the dining room." As I said this, though, his face looked sad, and he dropped his shoulders. I quickly followed up with, "I'll tell you what. I will see what I can do, but I won't promise you anything."

He perked up a bit and said, "Thank you for taking the time to listen to me." As he walked away, I couldn't stop thinking about how polite he was. I made it my mission to help him. I watched him work every day and could see how good of a worker he was, and how he always came to work with a clean shirt and uniform.

On my second to last cruise, I asked the office to send me a new dining room cleaner. They asked me why, and I told them I was going to promote the one I had. They told me I shouldn't make any changes while on board, as the dining room manager would likely not be happy when he returned. I said that I didn't care. It was clear to me that the young man deserved a break, and I wanted to help him.

Moving from dining room cleaner to busboy was not only a big deal, but it also meant he would get an increase of $200 per week. This meant a lot to him and his family, and it would change his entire life.

The last day before I was to sign off, we had a new dining room cleaner on board, so I was able to announce that night that Clarence was promoted to busboy. His eyes lit up with excitement, and he could not thank me enough. I told him not to let me down. I was giving him a chance, and he better not lose it.

I signed off the next day, and I had a good feeling inside. The next morning, I would fly to Alaska to pick up the ship in Ketchikan. I got all of my tickets and left for Miami Airport when the time came. My first leg of the journey was to fly to Dallas, Texas, then change planes and fly to Denver, Colorado, then a short hop to Salt Lake City, Utah, only to change planes again and fly to Seattle, Washington. After all of that, there was another change to Alaska Airlines to fly to Anchorage, Alaska, and after arriving in Anchorage, I would then board a four-seater plane and fly through the mountains of ice to Ketchikan. Believe it or not, I could do all that in one day. It helped, of course, that the time change kept making it earlier as I went west.

I arrived in Ketchikan and was met by the ship's agent, a nice young girl with a very pale complexion. She greeted me and I followed her to her car so we could drive to the hotel. I asked her if she knew of any good restaurants in town, not knowing at the time just how small Ketchikan was. I said I was starving, as I had been traveling all day without any food. None of the domestic flights served any food, and I didn't have time to pick anything up while running from plane to plane to catch my connections.

She told me that if we hurried, the restaurant in the hotel should still be open and they had good fresh salmon here. My mouth was watering at the thought of fresh salmon. Anyone would be hard pressed to find a better piece of fish anywhere than in Alaska—especially the wild sockeye salmon.

As we arrived at the hotel, I was collecting my bags from the back of the car, and she said, "I will go in and check your reservation and also ask if the restaurant is still open."

I followed close behind her. As I approached the reception area, she already had my key and paperwork in her hand. She knew I was tired and wanted to make this transaction as smooth as possible. As she handed me the key to my room, she said, "I spoke to the manager, and he said if you can go straight to the dining room, they will keep it open for you."

I thanked her, and as I shook her hand, she said, "The ship will arrive at 7:30 tomorrow morning. By the time they clear Customs, you should be able to board around 8:00, so I will pick you up at 7:45. Have a good night."

She turned towards the front door, and I headed into the dining room. I had the best salmon I have ever had. It melted in my month.

The next morning when I woke up, I looked out the window and saw the ship pulling into the harbor below me. So I promptly got ready and headed down to the lobby of the hotel. I didn't stop for breakfast, as I knew I could get some on board.

I joined the ship and spent the next six months on board as the dining room manager.

One night as we werc due to leave Juneau, Alaska, at 11:00 p.m. I noticed we had not even started up the engines. I headed up to the bridge to see what was happening. As I entered the bridge, I bumped into the captain. The bridge at night is a very dark area because the officers on the bridge need to see very clearly out of the windows; therefore, the bridge is always in complete darkness.

I asked the captain what the holdup was, and he replied, "We have a big problem, but if I tell you, don't tell anyone else. Follow me to my cabin."

We went down four steps and turned a corner to enter he captain's cabin. "Have a seat," he said. "Can I get you a lrink?"

I said, "No, I'm fine," to which he replied, "Well, if you lon't mind, I will."

He poured himself a full glass of scotch. "Now," he said, "you must promise me you won't breathe a word of his to anyone."

I promised, and he took a large gulp of his drink and proceeded to tell me what was happening.

"The Greek officers, including myself, have not been getting our insurance paid by the company back in Greece or the last three months and it is in our contract. We are not too worried about ourselves, but the coverage is for our families also, and the company has not paid into it. The insurance company in Greece has notified us of this situation and told us if it is not paid up to date, we will lose all insurance for our families.

"The officers called our New York office today and said if they don't pay all insurance and get the policy up to date by 10:00 p.m. tonight, that they would all go on strike and stop the ship. It is now 11:15 p.m. and they have not heard anything from New York so far. I will need to let the passengers know soon what is happening."

I said, "Captain, most of the passengers are asleep by now, so let's not wake them up and have them worried. Let's wait awhile and see what happens. We can always tell them we had engine problems or something tomorrow, and that is why we did not leave Juneau."

I soon left the captain's cabin. There was nothing I could do but wait, so I went off to bed to get some sleep. A while later I heard engines start up, and we started to move. I looked at my watch and noticed that it was 3:00 a.m.

I found out the next day that there was a phone call made to the bridge from New York at 2:30 a.m. to say they had paid the insurance up to date, but it took a phone call to Greece. They were nine hours ahead of us, and they waited until the offices were open there to call the insurance company to confirm the transaction before the chief engineer would give the order to start up the engines.

I should have known that this was a sign that the company was struggling.

A couple of months later, I was transferred to another ship sailing out of Tampa, Florida, going to the western Caribbean. On our way back to Tampa after a seven-day cruise, I was called to the bridge for a phone call from my office in Miami. I went to the bridge to take the call. My operations manager in Miami told me they planned to stop the ship from sailing back out of Tampa next cruise unless the company paid what they owed. He followed up by saying that they hadn't gotten paid for four months, and the amount was well over half a million dollars. They would have until noon in Tampa to pay up or they would pull all of the food and beverage staff off of the ship. He told me not to say anything to the staff and to continue the cruise as normal, and that they would come on board in Tampa.

After I hung up, the captain asked me what was happening. I would not have told him anything except for the fact that he had told me most of the story that he heard from his office. The captain said he knew it was not right, but if the company walked off the ship on Saturday, that a lot of good people would be out of work. I agreed with him, but at the same time, I questioned how long my company should wait to get paid.

The next few days I didn't sleep, and I'm sure the captain didn't either. We arrived in Tampa on time on Saturday, and I noticed several top managers from our Miami office standing on the pier waiting for the ship. After the ship docked and was cleared by Immigration and Customs, they boarded the ship and headed to the Food and Beverage Manager's office.

I joined them a moment later; the plan was to wait on board until noon while both offices were negotiating to come up with some terms that would work for both parties.

All of the passengers from the last cruise had disembarked, unaware of what was happening, but as the morning went on, the new passengers who were supposed to be boarding were being held up in the terminal.

Twelve noon came, and nothing had been resolved. The phone line from the Food and Beverage Manager's office was hooked up to the shoreline's, so we had a direct line to Miami. Two minutes after twelve, the phone rang. The food and beverage manager handed it to the operations manager, and after a few "yes" and "no" words, he hung up. He turned to us and said, "It's final. We need to gather all our staff and tell them we are leaving the ship in one hour."

At the same time, the captain was getting the same message from his office in New York. He started to gather all of his staff in one of the ballrooms to tell them what was happening. The food and beverage manager called Immigration from his office, notifying them of our decision, and letting them know we would be letting off over 100 crew members. Another manager was contacting the bus company so we could bus everyone to Miami, while yet another manager was speaking with the Personnel Manager in Miami to get plane tickets ready for most of the crew to fly home. Some others would be transferred to other ships. Every manager had a job to do and was ready to spring into action.

One hour later, we were unloading all of our luggage and going through Immigration and Customs. Two hours later, we were heading down the gangway, but not before I made a stop at the captain's room. I knocked at the door and a shallow voice said, "Come in."

As I entered his room, I saw he was slumped down n his chair, looking quite dejected. I shook his hand and aid it had been a pleasure sailing with him. He looked up it me and said he couldn't help thinking of all of the crew nembers who lost their jobs over it.

An hour later I was driving back to my apartment in Cape Canaveral, as I, too, was out of a job.

CHAPTER 21

My Last Cruise III

My final, last cruise started when I was at home in Ireland taking care of my parents who were both sick, a tough job that I do not recommend; however, I always did what I could for my parents. They were both on the mend and we were having a great Christmas together when the phone rang. My mom picked it up and said to me, "It's for you, Harry. Someone from America calling."

It was my friend, Tommy Moore. He was working for a cruise line as operations manager and they were about to take over the whole food and beverage operation. He wanted to offer me a job on board the ship as the food and beverage manager. I had been out of work for three months and was itching to get back; the offer sounded great and when Tommy calls, it's not common to say anything but yes.

I was soon back in Cape Canaveral and on board the Dolphin IV. It is the smallest ship I have worked on—it only has the capacity for six hundred passengers and two hundred and fifty crew. We had two days to change all of he food and beverage crew and train them. This included all of the kitchen staff, dining room staff, and bar staff before we took on passengers.

The last night before sailing, we served dinner for all of the office staff and their families. This was a good test for all of us to see how well we could put everything together. We had a couple of problems, but could fix them before we sailed the next day with a full ship.

After our first cruise, we had a surprise visit from the Health Department. They came on board in the morning and left later on that afternoon. We had failed our first public health inspection. One area we failed was the dish washing area. We had all new crew and they were not trained properly. Later that night, I went down to the pot wash area and helped the guys. There were two large Jamaican men and one skinny Haitian. As I rolled up my sleeves, I said to them, "It's not your fault, you were not trained what to do, so the first thing we need to do is wash all the floors and then empty the three sinks, clean them, and fill them with hot water." The first sink we filled with hot, soapy water, the second with clean, hot water, and the last with warm water with bleach (wash, rinse, and sanitize).

As I was helping them, I felt a hand on my shoulder pulling me back; it was one of the Greek officers. He said to me in broken English, "You're an officer. You don't wash pots and pans. Get out of here." I tried to explain to him that this was the best way to teach them. He ended up walking away, cursing in Greek.

After two hours, we had cleaned everything and stacked all of the pots and pans in their proper places. I told them this was exactly how to work every day; and they thanked me for showing them. Every day after that night when I passed the pot wash area, the guys greeted me with big smiles and the place was always clean and tidy. I had earned their respect. The Health Department returned for a re-inspection, and that time we passed.

The first year we had our fair share of problems. The ship never ran under full power. We had a problem with one of the boilers. This meant if we ran into some bad weather, we were always late arriving in port. Another problem when there isn't full power is the air conditioning never worked to its full capacity, either. The chief engineer would turn the air conditioning on wherever the passengers were on the ship. In other words, when the passengers were eating in the dining room, we would have cool air there, but when they moved to the lounges, the air would follow. As a result, the crew suffered. We had very little air in our cabins and the kitchen was always around 120 degrees. I don't know how the cooks worked all day there. We were constantly sending them ice water and salt tablets to keep them from getting dehydrated.

When we arrived late back to our home port of Cape Canaveral, it was all hands on deck to get the ship cleaned and ready for the next cruise. One job of the food and beverage manager was to go to the dock as soon as the ship was cleared from Customs with the chef and wait for the ood delivery trucks. One by one they would arrive and unload their trucks with large pallets of food and drinks. The chef and I would check all of the food with the invoice to make sure we had everything and to make sure the food was OK. Then a forklift truck would bring the pallets next to a large opening in the ship's side, and we would have a team from the kitchen and dining room load everything by hand and carry it down to the various storerooms, where the provision master would arrange everything in its proper place.

This would take all day. We would literally put on the last few items moments before we sailed. This happened every cruise, and we sailed two cruises every week. After a day in our home port, I looked forward to sitting down with a few cold beers, taking a hot shower, and hitting the bed for a well-earned rest.

After six months back on board, they promoted me to hotel manager, and after another hard day in Cape Canaveral, I was looking forward to my cold beer. I took a shower and put on my nighttime uniform, then headed up to the lounge for my well-deserved beer. I walked over to a group of cruise staff and sat with them. One of the girls said, "Harry, have you met Suzanne yet? She joined the ship today as our new Social Hostess."

"No," I said, followed by, "Nice to meet you, Suzanne."

Suzanne was a beautiful woman with dark skin, dark hair, light brown eyes, and a big smile.

She shook my hand and said, "Nice to meet you, Harry."

We started seeing more and more of each other and even sat at the captain's table together every cruise. Suzanne was a smart young lady. She was born in London, England when her father was working for IBM. He was a tall, handsome man with a dark complexion. He was from British Guiana, and Suzanne's mother was from Jamaica, but they had been divorced for several years. Suzanne moved to Canada when she was young and grew up there. She called Toronto her home.

We dated seriously, when out of the blue, Tommy Moore, the operations manager, called me on the phone. We were in Key West and he said he was leaving the company to go to another cruise line. He said he had mentioned to the Managing Director how I would be a good replacement for the job. I couldn't believe it. I had a chance to work ashore as the operations manager for the cruise line. It was too good to be true. I asked him when this was going to happen, and he said I would have to meet with the directors that weekend. If they were satisfied, I would work in the office the following week.

I was sitting outside at a café with Suzanne, and I told her the news. I could tell she was excited for me, but the look on her face said she didn't have high hopes that we would be together, and she didn't expect that we would be able to see each other again.

That weekend I made sure I had a clean white uniform on when I went over to the office. I was escorted to a conference room where there were several directors sitting around a large table. They took it in turn to ask me several questions, and after an hour, they asked me to wait outside the room for a moment. It was about five minutes, but seemed to me like hours. Then the door opened and I was asked to step back inside.

"Congratulations and welcome ashore," one director said to me. "You've got the job you will sign off the ship next cruise and start on Monday."

I couldn't wait to rush back to the ship to tell Suzanne, but was not sure how she would take it.

The captain and dining room manager had a party for me the last night of my cruise. It was bittersweet as I would see everyone every time the ship was in port twice a week, but it would not be the same as working side by side with them every day on board.

Suzanne and I met every home port after my new job started, and I was able to sail on board some weekends. Although it was nice, it wasn't the same as seeing her every day, so after a few months when I realized things were serious, I asked Suzanne would she get off the ship and stay with me on shore. She took little convincing. A week later, Suzanne and I lived together at my place.

We could still take some cruises, since part of my job was to take a few trips and inspect the ship and spend time with the captain and all officers. We would sail on the ship on Friday and return on Monday. Suzanne loved it because she would be pampered while on board. The first thing she would do was to book an appointment with the masseuse and sometimes the hairdresser. I would go to the bridge and meet the captain. We were treated like royalty every time we sailed. The chief purser would always give us the owner's suite if it was available, and most times it was. There would be some fresh flowers in the room along with a basket of fruit and some chocolate-covered strawberries. Suzanne and I would get to sit at the captain's table again. After each time we sailed, when the ship arrived in Freeport, the captain and I would play golf on the island and Suzanne would stay on board, sunbathing on the top deck. Life was good.

During my time as operations manager, the ship was still having its share of problems. Every time it reached home port, I would go on board and meet with the chief engineer to discuss any issues. I would meet up with him in his office, and he would give me an update on everything.

I was in charge of the entire ship's operations. In port, I would meet every manager and officer on board to see how the cruise went and to give them my support from the office.

One day, the chief engineer called my cell phone. Before the ship had reached port, he was concerned about something in the engine room, and wanted me to come on board immediately after the ship docked to see him. I could hear a quiver in his voice, which I had not heard before. I was concerned.

I immediately made my way down to the pier and waited. As the ship was maneuvering into the harbor, there were two tugboats, one at each end of the ship, pushing it towards the pier. I could see the captain on the bridge looking over the side, with a walkie-talkie at his mouth. Right next to him was the pilot, watching as the ship inched closer to the pier.

As soon as the gangway was lowered, I went through Customs and boarded. I headed down to the Chief Engineer's office. As I entered, he was sitting down at his desk with the blueprints of the engine room on the table.

Both he and his second in command were looking them over carefully, and muttering away in Greek to each other. They stopped as I entered the small room.

The chief engineer greeted me and said, "There is something I need you to see. Follow me to the engine room." I went with him down the long corridor and then through a watertight door. We climbed down a very steep ladder to the engine room. The noise and heat were unbearable. We then climbed over several large pipes and down another stepladder that led us to the bottom of the boiler room. The chief engineer stopped right in front of us; I could see two engineers staring at a large pipe with a big hole in it. The chief engineer said something to me in my ear, but the noise was so loud I couldn't make out his words. We both looked at the pipe. The water was gushing out of it and into the engine room. I could see they were pumping the water out, but the pumps were not working fast enough to take the water away as the engine room floor filled up.

The chief engineer turned to me again and pointed up in the air, so we turned and headed back the way we came.

When we got back to his office, he told me, "The large pipe with a hole in it was a pipe that took in salt water from the outside of the ship to cool the engines, and there was no valve to shut it off."

He added, "There is one thing we are going to try, and that is to surround the pipe with a box, and fill it with quick dry cement, and see if we can stop the water until we can replace the pipe."

He followed up by saying, "I will keep you informed throughout the day."

Later that afternoon, I went back down to the Chief Engineer's office to see how everything was going.

We both returned to the engine room and looked. The first attempt didn't work, so they were trying a second, larger box, placing it over the first one. The cement was not totally dry yet, and the water was still gushing out of the pipe, not as quickly as before, but still enough to be concerned.

It was 3:00 p.m., and we were due to sail at 5:00 p.m. All of the passengers were on board and unaware of what was happening below.

The entire time I was keeping the Managing Director in the office and the owners up to date with all that was happening.

I checked back again at 4:30 p.m. The engine room was filling up with water. It was over our shoes, and the water was still coming out of the pipe. This time I headed up to the captain's quarters, where I met the captain and chief engineer. I asked them both how bad it was, and they both looked at me and said, "Not good."

I replied, "Do you need me to cancel the cruise?" They both looked at each other for a moment, without a word spoken, but the expressions on their faces told me they both had the same thought. I turned to the captain and said, "Captain, if you don't think it is safe to sail, I will take your decision as final, and back you up with the head office and owners."

The captain replied, "We can make it," as he looked at the chief engineer. "I will have an officer on watch all night, and if we take it slowly, we can reach the Bahamas and get it repaired there."

He continued, "I have already contacted Miami, to send over the parts to the island tomorrow. They should be waiting for us at the pier in Freeport when we arrive."

The captain knew what the chief engineer and I knew, and that was how we couldn't afford to miss that cruise, and possibly a couple more. Losing all of that revenue, the owners would not be happy. At the same time, we had to think of the safety of the passengers and crew.

I looked over to the chief engineer, and he nodded in agreement, smiled at me, and said, "Yes, we will make it."

That afternoon, I stood at the pier as the ship pulled away, and slowly headed out to sea. I waved to the captain on the bridge and couldn't help but wonder what would happen if they didn't make it.

As the ship rounded the pier and headed out to open waters, I got into my car and drove down A1A, a highway down the coast of Florida, watching the ship as it disappeared over the horizon.

***

That night, I could not sleep. I arrived at the office early the next morning and went to my desk. I called the ship's agent in Freeport and asked him if he had heard from the ship. He replied, "Yes, the captain called an hour ago. He is running late, but should pick up the pilot around 10:00 a.m."

I called the ship and spoke with the captain. He said, "It was a long night. We were able to stop most of the water, and the good weather and calm seas helped." He continued, "We will get it fixed properly in Freeport. All the parts have arrived from Miami, and as soon as we dock, we can get he job done. However, we may be late leaving tonight and hat will delay us getting back to Port Canaveral tomorrow norning."

I was relieved. I went into the director's office and gave him the good news. The ship arrived back in Port Canaveral he next morning two hours late, but in one piece.

As far as the passengers and most of the crew, it was a normal, uneventful cruise. For me, though, it was the most tressful and worry-filled time in my life; I know I grew ome grey hairs that weekend.

One morning I was in my office and it was a busy lay All of the ships were in port and my phone would not top ringing. I picked up the phone, and the receptionist aid there was a gentleman waiting in the lobby to see me; assumed it was another salesperson. I would get several alls in to the office every day from salespeople who wished o see me. I asked her what he wanted, and she said, "Just o see you." I told her I was sorry I couldn't see anyone that lay. I was too busy with the ship in port. I slipped out of the ide door and made my way over to the ship.

The next week, also on Friday, the phone rang again. The receptionist said the same young gentleman was there o see me again, and I again said I was busy. She told me he said how he didn't mind waiting. After a couple of phone calls to the ship, I walked up to the lobby to see who he was, and as I entered the lobby, there were several people waiting. It was always a busy area on port days. At that moment, a tall, black man stood up. He was in an all-white officer's uniform, but I knew it was not our officer's uniform. He stretched out his hand to shake mine and said, "Good morning, Mr. Greenlee, you don't remember me, do you?"

I had to admit I didn't. I said, "Sorry, I don't."

He said, "I am Clarence, the dining room cleaner you promoted six years ago to a busboy. Now I am the Assistant Food and Beverage Manager on Carnival. I would not be here today if you didn't give me the chance all those years ago, and I just wanted to say thank you from me and my family. Thanks to you, my wife has a nice home and my kids will be able to go to college."

I shook his hand and said I was proud of him and all that he had achieved, and that I was happy to help; the rest was all his hard work. I wished him luck as he headed out the door.

He made a bad day turn into a great one. I will never forget that day and how he must have tracked me down to show me how far he had gone in his career. It's amazing how no one can ever know how they can make a difference in someone's life.

***

Six months had passed, and the ship was to spend a week or two tied up in Cape Canaveral for major repairs. I decided this would be a great time for Suzanne and I to get married. We could have all of our friends from the ship attend.

I asked the owner's permission, and they thought it was a great idea. It was settled that we would have the wedding ceremony and the reception on board the last night before the ship would sail with passengers.

We sent out 300 invitations, and my parents and brother planned to fly over from Ireland; my brother would be my best man.

Stacey in the office ordered all of the food, wine, and beer, and the chef who was due to go on vacation stayed on board and did all of the cooking, including baking the wedding cake. He said he would not miss it for the world. The ship's band said they would play for our wedding and the photographer said he would take all of our photos.

Our wedding day was spectacular. Suzanne looked stunning in her wedding dress, as did all of her bridesmaids. Her dad and stepmother came down from Toronto, as did her brothers and stepsisters. Her mother and her 90-year-old grandmother came as well. I believe everyone who was sent an invitation showed up, along with most of the officers and crew.

The chief engineer was frantically working on the air conditioning to get it right for our special day on board while the rest of the crew were setting up decorations and preparing the dining room and showroom. It was the greatest day of our lives, only made more special since we had all of our friends to share in it with us.

Suzanne and I did not take a cruise on our ship for our honeymoon. Instead, we flew out to Tahiti a week later and took a ten-day cruise around the South Pacific, including Bora Bora.

***

A year later, the owners decided to close down their cruise operations. The ship, although full, was not making money. It was old and in need of many repairs. They felt they couldn't put any more money into it, nor could they find the money to buy another newer ship. Although, they had talked about it a year earlier and were looking for one.

There was one more week to go till operations ceased, so Suzanne and I decided to go on the last weekend and sail with all of the friends we had made over the years. It was a sad time. Some of the crew would later get jobs on other cruise lines, some would go home, others would try to get work on land, but one thing was certain, and that was how we would never see each other again, at least not all in one place.

Monday morning, the ship pulled into Port Canaveral for the last time. All of the passengers disembarked, and then half of the crew. The other half would need to stay on board while the ship sailed down to Freeport. It would stay there until they figured out what to do with it. It would be too expensive to keep the ship tied up in an American port.

That night, around 5:00 p.m., the ship headed out to sea for the last time. The ship eventually wound up in the ships' graveyard. This was an area in Freeport where old cruise ships went to die.

I would see the ship one more time. About two weeks later, we were wrapping up everything in the office when the Chief Operating Officer called me into his office. He said, "I have two important things for you to do. One is to fly down to Freeport with the last payroll for the crew still on board."

"And the other?" I said.

He glanced over to one of the owners, paused a moment, and then said, "While you are on the ship, we need you to clear out the casino and take all of the money to a local bank, then get a transfer check and bring it back to us."

He went on to say how we still owned the ship, but in a couple of days, the bank would seize the ship and all of its assets. They needed to get the money off right then.

That night I called the ship and told the hotel manager of my plan. I asked him not to say anything to the ship's agent and to have the tour operator meet me at the airport. I did not want the ship's agent to know what I was up to as we still owed him money, and I could not get the money off of the ship if the agent informed Customs.

The next day I was flying from Orlando to Fort Lauderdale, then transferring to a smaller plane that would take me to Freeport.

I arrived in Freeport at 9:00 a.m., and after clearing Immigration and Customs, I walked outside to meet Mike, a tall, dark Bahamian I had known for some time. In fact, he and his wife had come to our wedding a year earlier. He drove me to the ship a few miles from the airport, and when I arrived, the hotel manager was waiting on the gangway. As I greeted him, I handed him the big brown envelope with the payroll in it (all of the crew members were paid in cash and in U.S. dollars). There was over $30,000 in the envelope. He told me that the casino manager and his assistants were ready and waiting for me in the casino. I knew I had little time; I had to get it all counted, then take it off of the ship to the bank, get it counted again, and get back to Cape Canaveral that same night.

We started with the nickel machines and then onto the dime machines, and lastly, the quarter machines. This took us all morning, and when we were finished, we had eighty bags—all about the size of a large bag of flour—full of coins that had all been counted. The next thing was to count the safe. That was a lot easier. Finally, the last thing to do was count all of the chips even though I was not taking them with me, as they were still part of the casino manager's report.

I called Mike and asked him to meet me in his truck at 2:00 that afternoon.

After we counted everything and had half of the casino floor covered with brown bags, we went and got some lunch with the captain and hotel manager. I asked the hotel manager if he could organize as many people as possible to help move the bags. He said he would have a team assembled at 1:00 p.m.

After lunch, the casino manager and I returned to the casino where there was a team waiting for us. After signing a few papers to verify the amount, I made a human line from the casino to the gangway and we started to move the bags. Mike had pulled his truck up to the bottom of the gangway, and I, with his help, arranged the bags into his truck. As we were filling up the truck, I could see the weight was lowering his truck closer to the ground. After the last bag was on the truck, we drove slowly to the downtown bank. Mike had already notified the bank that we were coming, and as luck would have it, the bank manager was a sister of Mike's.

We pulled up outside of the bank and she had several people waiting to carry the bags into the vault. It went quickly, and when the last bag went into the vault, the manager wrote me a check for $64,000. I thanked her and then Mike took me to the airport.

I returned to Port Canaveral late that night and brought the check to the owners the next morning. When I handed it over to them, all they said was, "Hmmm, was that all that was there?"

That was the end of my cruising experience.

CHAPTER 22

It's an Institution

Years after my days at sea, I was watching a film called *The Shawshank Redemption*, and there was a scene where Brooks, the old man who was the librarian in prison, was finally released. He soon learned he could not survive outside of the prison, as it was a strange place for him and he could not adjust to the outside after so many years away. He took his life while in his room. He hung himself from a beam in the ceiling. Later on in the movie, Morgan Freeman's character said to Tim Robbins' character, "These walls are funny. First you hate 'em, then you get used to 'em. Enough time passes, you get so you depend on them. That's institutionalized.

Life on the ship is very similar to that. On board, there is the same routine every day and everything is done for passengers, and much for the crew, too. Cabins are cleaned, clean towels are in the rooms every day, beds are made every day, meals are made, and there is a feeling of safety on the ship. There isn't really any awareness of what is going on in the actual world, and the ship becomes the crew members' world. Years ago, we did not have the communication that there is nowadays on the ship; there were no cell phones and no Internet back then.

One can go ashore every once in a while when in port and take a vacation once a year, and although it is exciting to get off of the ship for a while to see family, it isn't long before crew members begin to look forward to getting back on board again with friends. The outside world is not the world for these people anymore.

I don't want the idea to be out there that ship life is not great. As I said in the beginning, I had a blast and I would not be writing this book if I didn't have many good memories along the way. However, it was very hard to make that break away from ship life. When I did, it took me several jobs, moves, and years to feel normal on land again—whatever normal is.

I remember one Christmas Cruise when we were supposed to dock in Ocho Rios, Jamaica on Christmas Eve, and all of the Jamaicans working on the ship had bought all of their Christmas presents in Miami. They were excited to get off of the ship if only for a few hours to see their families. All of the other crew members were willing to work extra hours so their fellow crew members could get off of the ship in Jamaica. I remember it like it was yesterday. Even though it was some 20 years ago, the weather was so bad. There were heavy winds and rain as a freak storm hit us and was covering the whole island of Jamaica. The captain approached the harbor, and it was evident that he was going to have a problem docking the ship. He got closer to the pier and pointed the bow at the pier. The stern of the ship was pushed out by the wind, and the ship drifted further from the pier. He tried for over two hours to dock the ship, and at one point he was very close, but the wind picked up and pushed the ship away.

By this time, most of the passengers and all of the crew, including myself, were on deck watching the whole thing. There were a lot of my Jamaican friends beside me. They were waving at their families who had come to the pier to see their fathers, sons, brothers, and husbands. They were so close that they could shout to each other, but more and more it was looking bad, and finally the captain announced over the PA system:

"Ladies and gentleman, it is with great regret that I have to tell you I will not be able to dock the ship in Jamaica today, and for the safety of all passengers and crew, we will depart to our next port of call, St. Thomas."

I heard a boo sound coming from the deck above, and when I turned to look back at my Jamaican friends, their eyes were filling with tears. Grown men all with tears in their eyes were waving to their families as the ship slowly disappeared from the pier and turned out to sea. I had a lump in my throat and could feel tears filling up in my own eyes as I thought about how they would not get to spend time with their families this year as we returned to work.

I walked by the ballroom where the cruise director was addressing a large group of passengers and trying to put a schedule together for the next day at sea. A group of passengers were shouting at him, complaining that they were not getting to see Jamaica. They were so loud that no one could hear him over the noise.

At that moment, one guest went up on stage and grabbed the microphone from the cruise director and said in a loud voice to the disgruntled passengers, "Stop feeling sorry for yourselves. If there is someone you want to feel sorry for, it should be those crew members who won't get to see their wives and kids this Christmas. At least you are all here on board with your families." At that moment a large number of the passengers stood up and started applauding him. This went on for a good three minutes. The cruise director thanked him and went on with the show.

Later that night, the captain came down to the crew mess and stood in front of all of the crew. With tears in his eyes, looking especially at the Jamaicans; he apologized to everyone for not being able to dock the ship. I can tell you that few captains would have done that.

***

I worked with an Italian waiter for many years on the same ship; he was married, with no kids, and he had met his wife on board. She worked as a hairdresser and one year they went back to England to get married. After the wedding and a short honeymoon, he decided to return to the ship and his wife stayed in England; he said he could make and save quite a sizable amount of money by staying on the ship rather than going to work in England, and then he would get off after a couple of years and go home and start a family.

As long as I knew him, he would spend twelve to fourteen months on the ship. It seemed he didn't want to leave, and when he returned, he would do the same again. He was a good waiter and the passengers loved him. He had a great zest for life and his work, but at what cost to his wife? I remember one year he was actually excited to be going home to England, only to find him back on the ship only two weeks later. He looked different. The zest was gone. I had never seen him look so bad. I found out that when he returned home, he wanted to surprise his wife and arrived at the door of his house without telling her he was coming. He got to his house, took out his key quietly, and put it into the lock, but when he tried to turn the key, it wouldn't work. After a few moments, he gave up and knocked at the door. A stranger came to the door and asked him, "Can I help you?"

He said, "Who are you? This is my house," and the other gentlemen said there must be a mistake since they had purchased the house six months before from a lady. It turned out that his wife had sold the house and moved away, but he did not know where, and as he was a citizen of Italy, the house and everything was in his wife's name. He later found out she moved back in with her mother because she was lonely. They divorced later that year and he was still working on the ships when I left the cruise ship business.

Many people I have met over the years have not found it easy to transition from ship to shore and they end up back on the ships. I know of several people who have made it their lives and will most likely be on the ships until they are carried off in body bags.

One such person I met several years ago. His name was Mr. Frank Drummond, a real gentleman. He was born in Jamaica in the early 1900s and worked on a cargo ship that would sail from Jamaica to Miami carrying rum, bauxite, and coffee, along with clothing and other food to Jamaica, Cuba, and the Dominican Republic. Sometimes there were stowaways on the ship coming back from the Islands. The company was Eastern Shipping Corporation, and one owner was Mr. Frazer, the father, and his son, Lewis Frazer, who eventually provided all of the food, beverages, and staff for a now well-known cruise line, none other than Royal Caribbean Cruise Line. Back in the early 1970s, Mr. Drummond followed Mr. Frazer to the cruise ships and worked as a cabin steward and then as a head housekeeper in charge of the whole department. When he and I met, he was already in his eighties, but he would rise every day at 5:00 a.m. and I would see him around 6:00 p.m. still checking on his staff. He would go to sleep around 8:00 p.m. and get up the next morning and do it all over again.

He was in good health, although he had his selection of pills he would take each morning. He and I would meet for lunch up on deck and I would listen to his stories of how it was in the earlier days. I had great respect for him; he had been through a lot, and his face told the story. He was married and his wife lived in Miami. She would drive to the ship every Saturday to pick him up, and they would spend half the day together. She would bring him back to the ship around 5:00 p.m., kiss him on the cheek, and wave to him as he would climb the gangways, all the while shouting to him, "I will see you next week, honey." This had gone on for years since they were married for sixty years and it was obvious they were still in love and were both happy with the arrangement. They likely would have driven each other crazy if they were living together.

I remember one night I was just finishing up in the restaurant. It was around 1:30 a.m., and as I was making my way down the stairs to my cabin, I saw Mr. Drummond sitting on a chair in his pajamas; he was clutching a very old, tattered, black briefcase as if he didn't want anyone to take it away. I asked him what was wrong; he said he had to give his room up because the ship was oversold and the chief purser needed another cabin for some passengers. The chief purser told him to wait where he was and he would be back to find him a bed, but two hours had passed and no one had gotten back to him. I immediately went to find him another room and then I came back to help him to his room. As I was lifting him up, his briefcase fell and as it hit the ground it burst open and out dropped a bunch of pills and a pair of false teeth. I picked them up for him and saw to it that he was settled in for the night.

That was the last time I saw Mr. Drummond. I changed ships several times after that and never saw him again; he was definitely someone who was addicted to the institution of cruise ship life from his time on board. Years later, I heard from someone through an e-mail that Mr. Drummond passed away in his home in Miami. I could not get to the funeral; however, I prayed for him and his family that night.

To this day, if you ask anyone who has worked on a ship for a while, they will all tell you that it was not only the best time of their lives, but if they could, they would go back in a heartbeat, and that includes me. Some people say it's because we are all drawn back to the ocean because we all came from the ocean, some say it's because we spent so much of our younger life on the ship, some will even say it's destiny, but if you ask me, I believe it's magic. It's the magic of all of the great friends from all parts of the world, and because they become like family, along with the magic of the sights, sounds, and smells of the ocean, and the magic when standing on the top deck on a clear, starry night, staring up into the heavens.

It's the magic of the lighting striking the surface of the ocean way off on the horizon. And yes, long before Leonardo DiCaprio did it in the film, *Titanic*. I stood on the bow of the ship arms stretched out with just the railings preventing me from falling over, and the sun hitting my face, the wind blowing through my hair, looking at the horizon and then below some 60 feet to see the dolphins and flying fish jump out of the water just in front of the prow of the boat, and watching the ship cut its way through the blue water with white surf passing along the sides of the ship. It doesn't get any better than that.

Many passengers become institutionalized in a way. They are alone on land but take several cruises a year just to meet friends, and in many cases the ships become home for them. They get to know the crew and they become part of each other's family. I know of one middle-aged woman who had been married several times in the past and had taken several cruises with her husbands over the years. When she lost her last husband, she still loved to cruise; she had no children and all of her family had passed on, so, to her, the crew on the ship were her family. She had been on fifty-one cruises, and of those, twenty had been on the same ship.

***

Life on board the ships has given me some of the greatest memories I will ever have. Aside from the long hours and hard work, there were parties that went on all night, visits to many exotic places, but most of all, friendships built over the years. I am pleased to say that as I have gotten older, I still keep in touch with many of my cruise ship friends from all parts of the globe.

I have learned many things in my life, and have made many mistakes. At the end of the day, life is about family and the friends I met along the way.

Appendix

Department Heads

Captain: The person in charge of the whole ship. The captain is responsible for all of the passengers and crew and only answers to shore-side upper management.

Cruise Director: The person responsible for all of the entertainment onboard the ship.

Hotel Director: The person in charge of the hotel side of the ship, including food and beverages, rooms, etc.

Executive Chef: The person responsible for all of the food that is served on board the ship.

Food and Beverage Manager: The person who runs the whole food and beverage service on board, including all restaurants, bars, and room service, as well as any food service that may be offered on the private islands.

Dining Room Manager: There could be several on board who are responsible for the operations in each dining room.

Bar Manager: The person responsible for all of the drinks served on board.

Head Waiter: Depending on the size of each dining room, there may be a couple or several head waiters assigned to each dining room to assist the dining room manager.

Waiter: There are many men and women who work as waiters on the cruise ship, serving food to cruise-goers.

Busboys/Assistant Waiters: Their job is to assist the waiters in the dining room.

Chief Purser: The person in charge of all of the financial aspects of the ship.

Head Housekeeper: This person is in charge of all of the cabins and public areas of the ship.

Cabin Steward: There are many cabin stewards on board to clean the cabins every day.

Chief Engineer: This person is responsible for everything from the engine department, including air conditioning, water supply, heating, lighting, and keeping the engine running at optimal performance.

Casino Manager: This person is in charge of all of the casino tables and slot machines on board.

Gift Shop Manager: This person is in charge of all of the gift shops on board.

Hair Salon Manager: This manager is responsible for all of the beauty shops on board.

Shoreside Staff

Operations Manager: This manager is responsible for all of the ship's operations and represents all of the operations shoreside, in the home office.

Personnel Manager: This person is responsible for the hiring of all of the ship's personnel, including scheduling vacations and assigning what ship they will be on each cruise.

Ship Terms

Tender: A small boat that takes the guests from the ship to the shore, used when a ship is anchored offshore.

Gala Buffet: This is used to describe a large midnight buffet on board the ship where all of the kitchen staff can show off their talents; it usually happens once every cruise.

Gangway: A large platform that connects the ship to land, while in port, used for all passengers and crew to embark and disembark the vessel.

Galley: Another word for "kitchen" on the ship.

Bulkhead: This is the interior part of the ship that separates the metal hull from the inside of the ship.

Port: This is on the left side of the ship when facing forward.

Starboard: This is on the right side of the ship when facing forward.

Bow: The front of the ship.

Stern: The back of the ship.

Prow: The bulb shaped part of the front of the ship that is hidden underwater.

Bow Lines: Large ropes that hold the ship to the pier when docked.

Bollards: Short posts on the pier to which the ship can be tied.

Bow Trusters: Propellers at each side of the front of the ship to assist in docking the ship to the pier.

Stabilizers: Two large wings approximately 12 feet long on each side of the center of the ship that are deployed during rough seas to assist in making the ship run more smoothly.

Pilot: A person who assists the captain with docking the ship; each port has an expert pilot who knows the port entrance well, and he would board the ship a mile or so out from port and bring the ship into the harbor as well as assist in taking the ship back out of port.

Captain's Quarters: The area on the ship where the Captain's sleeps, his cabin and often his office in the same area.

C1-D1 Visa's: There were two stamps you needed in your passport, one was to enter into the United States and the second was to be able to work on the ship usually issued for one year from the American Embassy in your own country.

Printed in Great Britain
by Amazon

84315998R00138

CRUISING CONFESSIONS

MY ADVENTURES WORKING ON A CRUISE SHIP

This is a true story of my life working on a cruise ship, how I got started to all the exciting adventures I had. as you will see I found it very challenging but a great experience not many get to have, along the way I met some great friends from 35 different countries and languages whom with the modern communications we have today Im in touch with every day. An experience I will never forget and one I would love to share with you.

HARRY GREENLEE

Born in a small town in Ireland, Dalkey, Co Dublin I came to the United States in the early 80's worked on several cruise ship's for almost 16 years in Food and Beverage, traveling around the world for Royal Caribbean Cruise Line, Premier Cruise Lines and Cape Canaveral Cruise Lines. Started as a busboy in the dining room on the Great Song of Norway and finishing my Ship Career as the Operations Manager shoreside for Cape Canaveral Cruise Lines.

Became a U.S. citizen in 2000 Now happily retired living the American Dream in Auburn Alabama.

ISBN 9798489930765

9 798489 930765